I0110059

ADVANCE PRAISE FOR
A BODY MADE HOME

"Sometimes we have to create the language for the stories we need to tell. In this book, Marshall Green has done exactly that. This book is a victory not only in bravery and honesty, but in craft and form. *A Body Made Home* is a book that will help everyone who reads it to become more free. Let one of those people be you."

—ALEXIS PAULINE GUMBS, author of *Undrowned: Black Feminist Lessons from Marine Mammals*

"Kai Green has been one of the most dynamic writers alive for a while. This memoir cements them as something wholly different. I have stretched and laughed and wept over this book. There is no memoir alive as fleshy and radically theoretical as this offering. Green takes Barbara Christian's thought to a place that I've never imagined. This place, where the body is as worn and flexible as the theory we used to explore it, is so so black, and this black is so necessarily trans. We wouldn't know or feel any of this if the prose weren't so in the pocket. Kai has made a book feel like flesh."

—KIESE LAYMON, author of *Heavy: An American Memoir*

"As intimate an experience as holding Kai's hand and looking into his eyes, this book shares memories, passions, episodic emptiness—all in the creation of the self. As a Black girl in Oakland who became a trans masc university professor in New England, Kai travels worlds interior and bordered. All is grounded in love for their mother, both as a vulnerable lover, caretaker, and as an archetype Black Mama. A luscious journey to integration and recognition."

—SARAH SCHULMAN, author of *The Fantasy and Necessity of Solidarity*

"*A Body Made Home* is Kai Marshall Green's spell of becoming, a text that turns silence into song and wounds into portals. Here, Black trans love and queer kinship blaze against erasure. Enter this work and find a sanctuary where language remakes the world and the body learns to fly."

—E. PATRICK JOHNSON, author of *Honeypot:*
Black Southern Women Who Love Women

"In *A Body Made Home*, Kai Marshall Green offers readers an utterly compelling, utterly courageous memoir of 'be&comin'' trans, especially at a time when trans bodies, black trans bodies, are criminalized and legislated against. Descended from Audre Lorde's literary notion of 'biomythography,' *A Body Made Home* treats the stories of Green's body as always evolving, ever in a constant state of transition, and thus unstable as black, as gendered, as classed, as trans. This is a powerful, timely work of resistance and self-determination. I felt like I was reading the future. And I could not put it down."

—ALEXIS DE VEAUX, author of
JesusDevil: The Parables

A BODY MADE HOME

They Black Trans Love

KAI MARSHALL GREEN

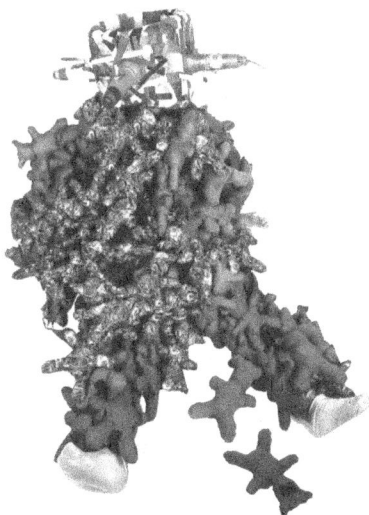

THE FEMINIST PRESS
AT THE CITY UNIVERSITY OF NEW YORK
NEW YORK CITY

Published in 2026 by the Feminist Press
at the City University of New York
The Graduate Center
365 Fifth Avenue, Suite 6200
New York, NY 10016

feministpress.org

First Feminist Press edition 2026

Copyright © 2026 by Kai Marshall Green

All rights reserved.

NEW YORK | Council on
STATE OF | the Arts
OPPORTUNITY.

This book is made possible by the New York State Council on the
Arts with the support of the Office of the Governor and the New
York State Legislature.

No part of this book may be reproduced, used, or stored in any
information retrieval system or transmitted in any form or by any
means, electronic, mechanical, photocopying, recording, or otherwise, without prior written permission from the Feminist Press at
the City University of New York, except in the case of brief quota-
tions embodied in critical articles and reviews.

First printing February 2026

Cover design by Dana Li
Cover art by James Welch
Text design by Drew Stevens

Library of Congress Cataloging-in-Publication Data is available
for this title.
ISBN 978-1-55861-322-5

PRINTED IN THE UNITED STATES OF AMERICA

I dedicate this book to Baby Girl and all the baby girls out there who struggle to find home in body. I dedicate this book to all the Black Bois and Black Trans Men who struggle to find home in masculinity, may it be the liberatory kind. May you too also come to know and love your divine femininity, it is your birthright. I dedicate this book to all childhood survivors, may we continue to heal ourselves and one another. May we all be&come more whole as we make our journeys toward healing. This book is over a decade in the making, it has taken time to be&come this text. May we all make the time for our greatest be&coming to be made manifest. With love for all of my readers, thank you.

♥ Kai Marshall Green

Contents

PART 3

Dear Reader,

Read this text aloud and silently, for multiple narratives are available for the feeling and the knowing on various registers. In the same way, you can read the text from start to finish or simply begin where your finger point takes you. There are many journeys to be had here.

—Black Trans Man

Baby Girl in kindergarten.

In the Beginning: Fast[1]

There was once a little Black girl, Baby Girl, who like to dig holes in the mud with the prickly twigs she find on the ground or sometimes she just use her own slender brown fingers for the diggin'. She like to feel the slime wigglin' pink worms buried just beneath the dirt's surface. She revel in the damp grit collecting underneath her fingertips. Dirt don't bother her. It's only that she know if she get too dirty she'll probably get in trouble—"You messin' up yo' school clothes!"

Baby Girl like to play with *the boys*. She like to take off her shirt and run around the yard like and with *the boys*. She don't think that she *a boy*, but she never told that there are certain things that she eventually have to be&come: an older Black girl, a Black woman, and then . . . The be&comin' a lesson. The be&comin' require a disciplining of the body. The be&comin' require a naming of the body, a naming that make what's hers both sacred and a burden, a naming that make what's hers not hers at all. Baby Girl sense this, because the be&comin' make her mother's, Black Mama's, smokin' hand shake, a nervous twitch. Black Mama want

Baby Girl to play and stay put, but Baby Girl's play often interrupted by . . . other things. Black Mama never want those . . . other things for Baby Girl, so she try her best to protect her baby's body.

Black Mama take Baby Girl to the doctor because she baby be growin' and bubblin' over. Her chest be&comin' breasts. Black Mama fret over not having more time. Too fast. Training bra now necessary armor for her kindergartener. Her baby's body be&comin' the ground upon which many battles gon' be fought. Black Mama already been a battleground body: She too be&come a Black girl and then woman. Black Mama's body already been made to bend and break and hold and birth some things that she rather not birth. She want to protect Baby Girl. She want to keep her whole and clean, but she know the world don't care about the sacred text that is her baby's body. The world too big and too cruel. The world also too small and too close, sometimes, like family.

Black Mama decide the only way to keep Baby Girl safe is to wrap her up in chains, chains like Jesus, Bible, silence, and secret-hush-hide. She long to keep Baby Girl from unsolicited touch, those who might harm her, some of the same people who harm Black Mama. But chains fail at slowin' Baby Girl's body from growin'. Those chains do create a distance though, between Baby Girl and herself, between her mind and her own body, which she for a long time not able to touch without the feeling of, *Dear God, if*

Black Mama and Baby Girl.

I do it again, please kill me! Baby Girl's battleground body be&come heavy, be&come this thing that she didn't ask for but inherit. Her body grow fast, and as much as Black Mama try to keep her, she cain't.

When it come out what happen that summer—three years after Baby Girl's body first start to show signs of be&comin' (she was eight)—when Baby Girl come to Black Mama and tell her of all the things that happen to her Black girl body, Black Mama respond with a question: "Did you like it?" Baby Girl confused by the question but instinctively respond, "No." She know that there's a right way to answer

3

that question so she don't get called fast like Cousin X, who's five years older. Baby Girl want more than anything to be good. She learn to love bein' good but never learn to love what it is she like, what it is that's good to and for her. What she like, she don't know how to name after that moment (she was eight). Healin' for Baby Girl come in the form of a learnin', learnin' how to name and ask for what she like, and a believin', believin' she deserve to have what she ask for.

Baby Girl be&come childhood survivor. When Baby Girl tell Black Mama what happen, nothing done to remove her from the situation, so she learn to live with it or rather have it live in her Black girl body that's always been be&comin' fast without her say so. She learn to appreciate the moments when Cousin X nice to her. Baby Girl bask in those sweet moments knowing they always gon' come with a side of cruelty. She never forget what it feel like to be slapped stingingly hard across her face by Cousin X. There ain't any bruises because Baby Girl's skin dark; the scars live beneath the surface and beyond the realm of visibility. There are no visible traces, the traces, the remnants of what had happened; that revealing take time.

Baby Girl go on to remember that summer (she was eight) every day for the rest of her life. After that time, migraines, depression, and "my stomach don't feel right . . ." be&come commonplace deep within her still be&comin' body. She try her best to reverse the stain of bein' fast. She be&come so good. But good not free, and discipline don't provide protection. Baby Girl's and Black Mama's bodies disciplined, but it's rare they ever protected. Black Mama want to keep Baby Girl safe, but body cain't be disciplined into safety.

Baby Girl's tale is not just her own, it is also Black Mama's "my stomach don't feel right . . .", aunties' "I don't remember. I won't remember. I refuse to remember," and cousins' whimperings after Grandma's whippin' belt come out, pants down, bent over the same bed Grandma make them kneel and pray at every morning. There are so many Black Girl battleground body stories to recount, and the body count continues to grow.

Baby Girl want to be free. Baby Girl want to crack up laughin', and she do, even if cousins do tease her about her gap. Baby Girl a feelin' baby. Baby Girl want to feel good. Baby Girl want to know if Jesus is real. Baby Girl a questionin' baby.

"The moodiest of *all* my babies," say Black Mama.
"She sensitive!" say Auntie G.

Baby Girl be&come. She be&come bigger. She be&come teenager. She be&come athlete. She be&come writer-poet. She be&come thief. She be&come strong enough to keep herself safe. She be&come traveler. She be&come boarding school kid. She be&come Born Again Christian going door to door askin' people, "Would you like to accept Jesus into *your* heart today?" She be&come baptized two times,

5

two times Born Again Christian. She be&come a Quaker leadership camp kid. A Black weirdo. A private school kid. An Oakland public school kid. She be&come smart and special. She be&come educated. She be&come from Deep East Oakland. She like Dru Down, Too Short, and Tupac, but Lauryn Hill and Donny Hathaway will forever be her ear's heart.

She like ridin' without a seatbelt on the passenger side while leanin' so far back in the clean seat of the classic car Daddy bring home that will, after two days, never be seen again. She be&come "I like spliffs . . . the side effects of graduate school." She be&come part of a wine-and-cheese academic world. She be&come stud after she practice femme and feel like she just cain't breathe. She be&come bald-headed femme on Halloween and decide to stay there.[2] She be&come stud again only softer this time. She be&come. She be&come "That ain't my name no more!" She be&come they and them, he and him.

She unbe&uncome over and over again too. She unbe&uncome Mama's Baby Girl, her only girl. She be&come Mama's Baby Boi, Black Boi, Black Trans Man, her third son; still the baby though. Black Mama always want a girl baby that grow to be woman, but she Baby Girl grow to be a Black Boi and a Black Trans Man. A lot like Daddy but not when he *on that stuff*. Though sometimes in the unbe&uncoming Black Boi be a lot like Daddy when he *on that stuff*, searching for some out-of-this-world high to hold on to.

6

Still image from the *A Body Made Home* short film series, 2023.

Baby Girl got a soft spot for Black Mama. She want to protect her. She be&come basketball scholarship kid. She be&come 5'10" at twelve. She be&come a silly awkward Black girl poem. She be&come misunderstood. She be&come cutter. She be&come "Get out!" She be&come model and token Black. She be&come Black radical-scary, a threat to white folk and their institutions. She be&come so in love with love, but it don't ever last.

She be&come "What happen if you take a poor Black kid and give them what they deserve?" She be&come to know the unfairness of it all. She look up to the hills to see the mansions peer down and surround her Deep East Oakland flatlands. She throw it up, all the words they try to cut from her tongue. She cain't stop sayin' it the way she do. And he the same way too. Black Girl and Black Boi, Black Woman and Black Trans Man be&come they, and this is a story of they Black Trans*[3] love and loving as it perpetually be&come done and undone.[4]

PART 1

Perhaps home is not a place but simply
an irrevocable condition.
—JAMES BALDWIN, *Giovanni's Room*

Home is memory, home is your history,
home is where you work.
—TONI MORRISON

Black Trans Man sits on the porch of his childhood home, Black Mama's house, holding an old photograph of Black Mama, Brother 1, and Brother 2, 2018. Photo by Texas Isaiah.

CHAPTER 1

Home

Home 1. [Noun]: *Home is a four-letter word.* A language. Something that you speak. Something that you write. Something that you write to. Something that was. Something that is not. Something that never was. Something that you still long for. Something that you don't believe in. Something that you want. Something that you want to believe in. Something that you pray for. Something that is connected to other things. Something that is its own thing. Something out there. Something in here. Something you forget. Something you lose. Something you lost in. Something lost in you. Something you find. Something you have. Something you re-remember. Something you remember with fondness and a glimmer of cocoa skin sitting atop a shoulder of sun in the midst of the coldest New England winter ever. Something you dream. Something you choose. Something you bear. Something you touched-touch. Something you won't ever return to. Something you get kicked out of. Something you move away from. Something that be&come. Something that unbe&uncome. Something imagined. Something promised. Something that is not what it sounds like. Something

13

that is exactly what it looks like. Something that is here. Now. Nowhere. There. Then. Never and always-elsewhere. A word. A gap to fill the insatiable empty [. . . not word . . .] between us . . . words lie.

Home is a four-letter word: "Mama."

Home is a six-letter word, arms reaching out and up, calling out, "Mother!"

Home 2. [Noun; proper noun]: *A person.* Someone you write to. A people. A bone. A break. A stop. A bend-curve. Mama and Mother are the same. Mama and Mother are not the same. Mother loves to. Mama hates to. But does it anyway cause Mother said so. Mama is a person. Mama is a word. Mama is a Black woman. Baby Girl Mama. Black Mama is . . . still searching for a name to hold all that she be&come.

Black Mama is not always a person but always Mother. Black woman is not always a person. Black Mama live in a world that don't see her but through desires of they own wants and greeds.

"Mother, get on yo' knees and hold me, please!" pray the pastor in his office just before Tuesday night Bible study and a firm squeeze; neither hug nor handshake. She will only say what it was not when she, Black Mama, was someone's Baby Girl. He did NOT make them pray prayers that made her stomach ache up in knots. It was the food, musta been the food. She will words to make herself believe it was NOT what it felt like . . . unholy. Pastor-teacher touch god and touch her God. Her God is not what Pastor-teach(h)er. Pastor taught her then that what was holy was not to be known through the affirmation of her own belly churn. In between her was only for the touching, not for the feeling. And she believe in Pastor god, not her own, no matter how much truth would be told. She believe in Pastor prayer on account of some miracles that had come and gone years ago. She learn to ignore the rumble of her own belly even though, since then, she always been hungry. An insatiable gap, word, distance [. . . not word . . .] between how Mama holds Mother and Baby Girl held and Baby Girl hold, "I cain't hear what my own body say no mo'!"

Pastor and other elders of the church who done had enough of their own Baby Girls and Boys too, they turn to her till prayer done just about worn through both her knees and throat. Burn.

Dear God,
make me. clean. and white. and pure. and pretty.
and loved.
Love, [. . . a word . . .]
Mother/Mama

Love is a word, and Black Mama want to hold it so bad. Black Mama do what Black Mama will. Black Mama don't never and always get what she want. Black Mama will don't always align with what Baby Girl want or with what she want for Baby Girl. What she would have wanted for Baby Girl. Roots all reaching and a-crossing and a-grasping. They tryin' to coalesce around a thing. A person. Not a person. Body capture. Always wanted. To stop that which is. Always was. Keep slipping out its grasps. Growing up. Down and outward. Toward and away from. Simultaneous. Slip don't mean fall. All at once. All together and at different speeds. Alchemy. It's how she imagine herself to be alive in a world that sometimes only see just above the surface. Not skin. Not flesh. Surely unknowing roots. Reaching. Stretching. Building patiently. Stressed out in believing. Mama get confused in Mother. Mother who is holding too many and all things. Worlds are made of the [. . . word . . .] gap between here and then. Time. Space. Trauma. Joy. It gets passed around. Down there. Underneath the ground where the bristly tree limbs braid themselves into one another. Touching. Mothers. Mama. A word. A body. [. . . not word . . .] to be&come (re)called.

Home is a two-word command: "Hold me!" Pastor say to Baby Girl . . . Baby Girl say to Black Mama . . . Black Mama say to Daddy . . . Daddy say to outside and his Mama (Grandma). Outside and their Mamas (Grandma and Granny) say to Jesus [. . . not word . . .]. Black Mama and Baby Girl the only ones who say, "Okay." They reach out they bodies in this chain of words, this time, not for all time, not even every

Black Mama, 1970s.

time. But this time was for a long time. Roots be pattern, tethered to the rotation of what is magnetic. Not the same as what is true or untrue, just the source that compels. Pulls at the insatiable distance between [. . . word . . .].

Home is a relationship, a bond, a root that go down deep underneath. Gravity holds them down.

Home is a seven-letter word: gravity.

"Okay." She reach out her body in this chain of words. this time. not for all time. not even every time. but this time was for a long time. roots be pattern tethered to the rotation of

17

what is magnetic. not the same as what is true or untrue. just the source that compels. pulls. the insatiable distance between [. . . word . . .].

Mama be&come home, always, at least for a little while, until babies come through and breathe on they own. Air, not water. You can only breathe underwater when you at home in Mother-Mama.

Home is a four-letter question: "Mama?"

Baby Girl ask, feeding her developing terror of being wrong and ignoring her own feelin' of knowin' right: "How you know our Jesus the right Jesus?"

Black Mama deep sigh and silence. Baby Girl feel. She stare out the back-seat window while picking at an old scab. Once removed, she chew on it, savoring the metallic-dirt-blood flavor of her own making, waiting for Black Mama to say something. The blood-sucking mollifies her uncertainty. She see Black Mama face through the rearview mirror, eyes forward.

Black Mama say, "I don't know. Just hope," and "Some questions, Baby Girl, only faith can answer, and prayer."

Baby Girl unsatisfied but don't ask her about it again. She figure Black Mama must not know either but take some small comfort in Black Mama belief, even in the not knowing. Black Mama believe what might not be true. And tell Baby Girl as much, though she never say the words, "Santa

Claus ain't real." She let Baby Girl have dreams until they sour or blossom on they own. But Baby Girl latch on to Black Mama. Black Mama god. Black Mama prayer. Black Mama memory.

Home is a confession: "Mother! Ooooooooo, Mama!" Brother 2 about Brother 1. Baby Girl about Cousin X and the others . . .

In tears, they latch on to Black Mama until home be&come a two-word command: "Get out! 'Cause I said so."

Home is a relationship, a bond, a root that sometimes don't take you nowhere. But where it is disconnected, where underneath the ground it rests, slowly be&comin' some-thing else: dust. 'Cause it got nothin' to wrap itself around. It be free, unheld and unholding.

Home is a six-letter word: Breath. Inhale.
And then a seven-letter word: Breathe.

Home is a body. made. Home is an incomplete exhale, a reluctant "Okay." She splay out her body in this chain of words. this time. not for all time. not even every time. but this time for a long time. roots be pattern tethered to the rotation of what is magnetic. not the same as what is. was. true or untrue. just the source that compels. pulls at. the insatiable distance between [. . . words . . .] a body make.

19

There is the body they born into, and there are the bodies they create and encounter along the way. The first home Baby Girl rest in is Black Mama belly. Black Mama a homebody, a body that only seek to be in one place, home. House, she buy it to have her own home, outside her body when she just twenty-one. Her body be&come home to her babies for a while but never fully hers. She daughter, root attached to Mama's Baby, Papa's Maybe.[1]

Black Mama can only be home for a little while until babies come through and breathe on they own, air not water. You can only breathe underwater when you at home in Mother-Mama.

Home is a seven-letter word: gravity.

Down. So down she cain't get up. Feet can only keep her here. Black Mama fine with stayin'. But she be&come home to a baby who don't have feet. Baby Girl got wings, and though Black Mama know flyin' dangerous, she don't dare cut her baby wings lest home be&come a six-letter word: prison. She don't want that home for Baby Girl, she already know that home for herself. Not a metaphor, she indeed given three days to be home *in prison*. That's where Daddy at most of the time, and that's where he stay the whole time Black Mama hold home in her body for their baby.

They gonna go see Daddy in San Quentin. They plan this trip for months. Letters get sweeter and sweeter and seem to come more frequently as the date approach.

And when I get home, we will hold hands and walk on
the beach, and I will whisper sweet nothings in your
ear ... and Baby, life gon' be good n' sweet. Let me tell
you how I'm gonna cook for you and dress our baby in
the mornings and do her hair ... OOOOh baby I'mma
make life so sweet for us. I'mma be yo' man, Godly
man, worldly man. I'll only have a beer every now and
again ...

Black Mama, she feelin' in love. She open, open to Daddy's
words, his vision, and his dreams. They her dreams too,
dreams to be in love and feel safe, to feel danger and laughter but not know pain. Black Mama believe things gon'
change. She pray. She pray. And sometimes, sometimes she
just stay at home, too, through with *The Church People* and
all their whisperin'. They don't know a damn thing about
love and prison!

Love when yo' man get locked up and leave you alone with
the most beautiful letters that only make you want more of
that dream you cain't touch. And them Holy Rollers don't
know nothin' 'bout passion, heat kind of passion, the kind
you feel when you lock eyes with a person, somebody, and
in an instant, realize it's not just a person but *your* person.
And suddenly Black Mama breathe fully thinking, *God done*
finally come through!

That's what she feel when she first hear Daddy bass line.
He stand up there to the right of the choir just behind the

Black Daddy playing bass guitar in Susanville Prison, 1972.

drum stand. He playin' to Black Mama, but people think
he must be playin' to God. Black Mama start to feel it, and
the beat start to get faster, and the bass line start to speed
and swang. Black Mama cain't help but jump up out her
seat; jump up, straight up in the air. Black Mama don't do
fancy footwork, she just jump up and down, up and down.
And a ring of old Black women in white who smell like

clouds of baby powder and peppermint sticks glide over and build a circle round her. And Black Mama, she just be goin'. Cryin'. Screamin'. Achin'. Breakin'. The old women, collectively called *The Mothers*, watch one another with hawk-eyed senses as they bend. Hold. Move. Dip. Creating a kind of syncretic waltz, circling round Black Mama's leaping body. *The Mothers* keep Black Mama safe while she go through her *Holy Ghost* catchin' journey. The *Holy Ghost* come through Daddy bass line. It do, and that day a lotta folk get *happy.* Afterward, Daddy, he go outside and smoke a joint, lean his head against the back door of the church, facing the sun, just waiting for the time to go back and play another round. Black Mama inside pretendin' to listen to the sermon, but really all she want is more *Dun Dun Dun Dun Dun Dun Dun Dun Dun Dun Dun Dun DUNNNNNnnnnnnnnnn . . .*

Dear Daddy,
I miss u. I love u. I wint to the parch. Saw the moon in the stars. After dark. Close my eyes and dream of you. Black Mama say we get to see you soon.
Love,
Baby Girl

Letters hold memories, memories of both the future and the past. Baby Girl fall in love with Daddy words through

Black Mama voice. Black Mama read his letters to her as bedtime stories. Daddy sometimes attach drawings that a talented cellmate sketch. This make Baby Girl think of cartoons, and she really like those. She imagine herself and Black Mama and Daddy in a cartoon world. Pain never last long in cartoon world. Healing is inevitable because there is always another episode, and whatever happen before seem to no longer be important. In real life, Baby Girl remember everything, even the things she long to forget, like *prison* and *scars*.

They family touch they dreams though too, sometimes, Black Mama, Daddy, and Baby Girl. Like that one afternoon they make a picnic basket and head to Alameda Beach. They sit on the sand, eat snacks, and they taaaallk, and they laaaaugh. Black Mama and Daddy love each other so deeply because they fall in love with each other's dreams and ideas. Sometimes they imagine something that none of them actually ever experience, an easy-breezy love, where husbands work and mothers care for children and house, *a good Christian household.*

But even if Baby Girl parents' dreams normative, they themselves are not. They both rather queer figures. Black Mama, a sex-positive (heterosexual), Scrabble loving, Christian social worker. Daddy, a musician, sometimes pimp-like, addict, church choir and basement playin' bass man. Black Mama describe Daddy as an afro that fall

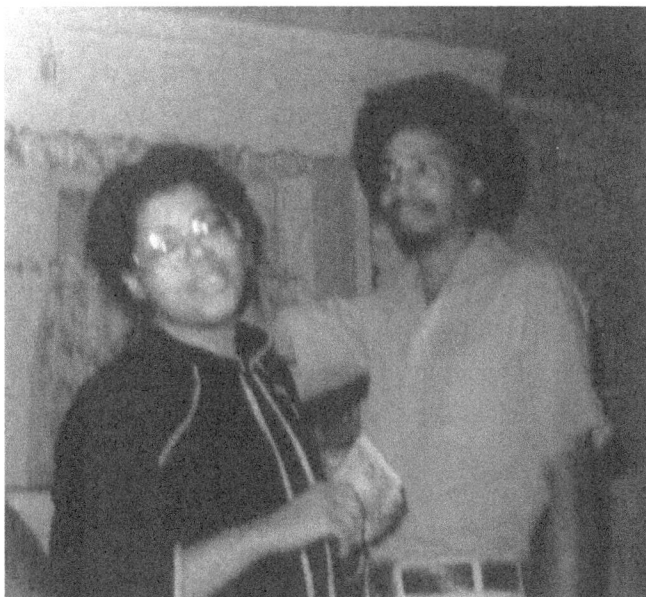

Black Mama and Daddy, 1970s.

with the wind. It never keep its shape. Daddy and Black Mama the same cinnamon brown skin tone. Daddy tall and skinny. Daddy particular about the waves in his hair and the creases in his pants. Daddy neat and particular. Black Mama church-girl pretty. Black Mama can wear a hat and rock some shoulder pads like nobody business. She not neat like Daddy though. Daddy keep his clothes on hangers and folded, while Black Mama keep her clothes in piles like little mountains. Baby Girl like to play in them, climb them, bury herself in her mother's closet, which was never bound by any door.

Anticipation bubblin', Baby Girl about six years old, and she know how to tell many lies while holding bundles of secrets, like sticks being collected for an inevitable burn.

Black Mama say, "What's your address if anybody ask you?"

Baby Girl respond with glee, "4900 Daisy Street!" She know Grandma address is what they need to use. Where they live, the schools ain't too good, and Black Mama want Baby Girl to have some opportunities. Black Mama use Grandma address for Brother 2 to go to the same school ten years before too.

What good are wings without a sky?

Black Mama say, "I'm writin' you a letter sayin' we goin' to visit your ___ in the hospital. They sick."

She don't want Baby Girl school to know that Baby Girl daddy in prison, and they finally goin' to see him. A three-day trip. The train ride to . . .

Daddy.

Daddy: a five-letter word that don't mean home.

Black Mama say, "Daddy, a two-word hope: *I wish . . .*

> *. . . I wish he would come home after payday. I wish he believed he deserved me. I wish I believed he deserved me. I wish we could make a home. I wish my home could hold him. I wish my home was more than a dream. I wish I had some help. I wish he would choose me instead of drugs . . .*"

Black Mama teach Baby Girl that *I wish* a declaration, a statement of faith. It could indeed *be&come* somethin' home could hold, but it never do, not for long anyways.

The train ride to San Quentin filled with hours of *Go Fish* and *tic-tac-toe*. They carry a picnic basket filled with food for the weekend. They only allowed to bring certain things. Black Mama bring it all. Mostly it seem to be fried chicken though. For those three days, they be together. They lie in the dull bluish-gray trailer, just laughin' and flirtin'. It is. Hot. Dry. Glaring. Stinging. Heat. The guards come by every hour for a roundup to remind them that they are in a prison and Daddy is just another number.[2] Daddy always be findin' a way, though, to do somethin' that he not supposed to be able to do. Sometimes that's where Black Mama say Baby Girl get her wings. That's why she want Baby Girl to have space, 'cause without space, she might easily fall into a trap and be like Daddy in prison, always searching for *free.*

Somehow, Daddy arrange to have his brother Uncle T come out to the yard. Baby Girl meet Uncle T behind a gate. Outside, it is. Hot. Stiff. Thick. Heat. They outside but not *free*. The fences so tall, no way to get over or under. Baby Girl reach for Uncle T's hand, and the tips of their fingers barely touch, but Baby Girl feel the sandpaper like scratchiness of Uncle T's skin. He bask in Baby Girl small fingers lightly tracing his own. They meet through the wire, walkin' together a few steps before a guard come by sayin', "Don't

27

touch!" Uncle T smile at Baby Girl, Black Mama, and Daddy. He turn, walk away, and fade into the heat. A family reunion underneath the watchtower.

The days go by quickly and when they leave, Baby Girl cry and fall to her knees:

> *". . . I wish we could stay here in prison with Daddy. I wish we could take Daddy home. I wish we could take Uncle T too. I wish Black Mama would say somethin' . . ."*

Black Mama silent on the train ride home. There ain't no card games. Just a deep holding of breath. Heavy. Breaking. Aching. Stiff.

Baby Girl close her eyes and dream of cartoons and Daddy and Black Mama and the beach and love until they finally back home. Next day she got school, and Black Mama got work.

"Remember where you went this weekend? To visit ___ in the hospital. They sick." Black Mama cain't bear eye contact today. She don't face Baby Girl when she talk 'cause she don't want Baby Girl to see her cry. Baby Girl pretend not to see 'cause she know cryin' make Black Mama mad. She don't like no tears. She cain't bear Baby Girl tears. So Baby Girl don't get whippins like other kids. Black Mama just tell

Baby Girl she disappointed, and Baby Girl cry for hours, so overcome with guilt. Baby Girl come here carrying feelins.

She nod to assure Black Mama she ain't gon' forget. That lie ain't difficult to remember. But years later when *Nice White Woman English Teacher* ask her why she all blues, and she say, "Nothin'," but write a poem about a girl with a scream that no one hear, Nice White Woman English Teacher say, "You're gifted, keep writing!" Baby Girl be&come obsessed with writin' herself away from where she at. She get good at carrying heavy. Sometimes she write it down. Black Mama give Baby Girl a journal long before she could read or write. She tell Baby Girl to put her feelings on those pages. Black Mama say she always believe Baby Girl gon' be a poet or a flautist. But when Baby Girl come home from kindergarten and tell Black Mama she want to be an artist when she grow up, Black Mama cry out, "Oh, no! Not a starvin' artist!" So Baby Girl decide instead to be&come cancer researcher. She don't want to be hungry, and she don't want to be poor.

Baby Girl be Black Mama's *poem.* Baby Girl be&come home for Black Mama. Sometimes Black Mama get sick . . . *a lot* . . . Baby Girl learn to hold Black Mama tenderly.

Home is a six-letter word: holder. Home is a five-letter word: women. Home is a six-letter word: Aunty.

Aunty G and Black Mama are sisters. Many confuse Aunty G and Black Mama 'cause they look alike and have matching Jheri curls, French rolls, and wigs. Aunty G is home.

Aunty G and Black Mama, 2000s.

Aunty G is home for Black Mama. Aunty G is home for Black Mama secrets and tears and dreams and manic episodes. Aunty G is home for sisters' babies, brothers' babies too, and that little kid from up the street, and her own babies. Aunty G is home.

Home is a seven-letter word: protect.

Aunty G got roots and wings. Baby Girl only born with wings, though she s'posed to be a home like Black Mama and Aunty G.

Home is a six-letter word: broken. Home is a five-letter word: story.

There're things Baby Girl remember and things she don't. The things she don't remember don't bother her, she just make them up. But sometimes what she make cain't hold nothin'; like Black Mama, home don't always keep secrets so safe.

Home is inside, a four-letter word: body. Baby Girl may not have much, but she got body. Her body will be made to hold home in spite of her "No!"

But there come a day when Baby Girl can breathe both air and water, when Baby Girl can both walk and fly, a day when *body* be made another four-letter word returning to her, like a name, just on the tip of her tongue, be&coming, whole-home. And when she get there, they discover home again anew, a four-letter word: *love.*

Love, like the cotton-candied cloud of old Black women in white, shielding Black Mama as she catch the Holy Ghost. The right to remain protected and loud as she want as she lose it. Loose it. That's how God show up in Black Mama. She safe to lose and loose it in that sanctuary. Many a Sunday somethin' just catch a hold of a person, and they cain't help but break free. Sometimes a person take off like a rocket, sprinting up and down the church aisles. Baby Girl try to join in once, but Black Mama tell her, "Stop playin' with God!"

Maybe the one who caught the spirit lose her hat, her wig, or maybe her makeup flow down her cheeks in trails of

Still image from the "A Body Made Home" short film series, 2023.

tears. A sight to witness, a sacred time. No one laugh, and no one judge. The women only come and hold a tight circle round the one who caught: a choreography of survival in a place like Deep East Oakland, with Daddy in prison, three babies at home, and a full-time job with a full list of clients all needing Black Mama to show up. All the while, Black Mama still carry some trauma from the past that will never be talked about. Black Mama say. Granny say. Grandma say. Her mama say, "Take it to Jesus." *The Mothers* cain't always hold Black Mama, bear the weight of it all. They cain't always keep Black Mama from the pain, but on Sunday mornings, Tuesday evenings, and Friday evenings too, they provide a temporary space for relief, for letting go, for being and going crazy, for screaming, for wailing, for crying out in pain and in gratitude. That ring of old Black women hold that circle round Black Mama, who they cain't always protect, but there's something about, about that name, ~~Jesus~~ freedom, about the freedom to be wild, to lose and loose it, and for a moment in that sanctuary, losing it for Black Mama is all right.

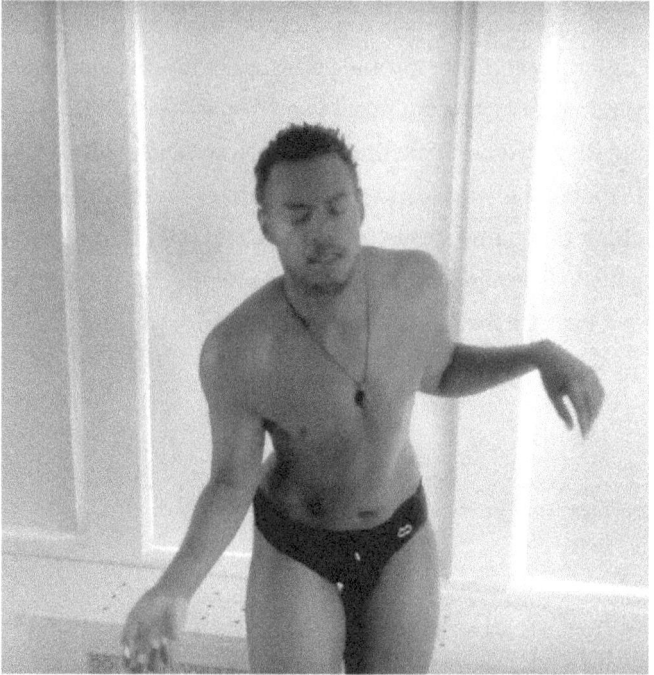

Still image from the *A Body Made Home* short film series, 2023.

CHAPTER 2

Losing It

*Traumatized by systematic terror and brutality,
some black people manifest what I call phenomenal
madness, severe unwieldiness or chaos of mind
producing radical crises of perception, emotion,
meaning, and selfhood.*

> —BRUCE LA MARR JURELLE, *How to
> Go Mad without Losing Your Mind:
> Madness and Black Radical Creativity*[1]

L **ost [Adjective]:** *Cain't find. Not winning. Misplaced.
It happened. It can happen again.*

Losing [Adjective]: *Not winning. To misplace. To cain't
find. It don't stop. The slip and the fall.*

Lost. Like losing faith.

Lost. Like finding herself in his dream.

Be&come her night-terrors.

Lost. Like lights off. Cain't see.

Follow a whisper.

Find me.

Lost. Like Baldwin say,

it never sleeps—that terror which is not the terror of
death (which cannot be imagined), but the terror of
being destroyed . . . and I'll never be found again.[2]

Lost. Like it's gone and cain't be found.
Lost. Like they here but cain't find they way there.
Lost. Like you over there.

🐦

Baby Girl always lose things. Keys. Shoes. Toys. She like to
spend her days riding her bike back and forth, up and down
the concrete sidewalk. She allowed to go three houses to
the right and three houses to the left, but sometimes she
ride around the whole block, and Black Mama never know.
Sometimes her and the neighbor kids make ramps with the
bricks and plywood that seem to always be piled on the side
of everyone's houses. Jump! She love to jump the ramp on
her bike but not on her roller blades, that's how she break
her wrist the first time . . . Sometimes when she outside just
by herself, she play alone with the plants. There's a pear
tree, blackberry bushes (they call 'em *sticker bushes*), a few
different kind of evergreens, sour grass that all the kids
love to chew on, and a star jasmine bush spread wide across
the front of they brick house. Sometimes Baby Girl take
the flowers and stems from the star jasmine and pretend
the sticky white liquid oozing from the plant is the cure
for cancer. She like to pretend a lot. She do a lot a dreamin'
right there just in front of they house. Black Mama have a

flex day every other Monday, and sometimes she let Baby Girl skip school to stay home with her. One Monday, they make a clubhouse on the porch with sleeping bags, they play jump rope, Skip It, and Hula-Hoop. Right there on that porch anything possible, and everything easy to find 'cause the porch ain't that big.

But inside they house, it be deep, wide, dark, ever-expanding, ever-collecting, always gathering more things. Things get lost inside they house.

Home be piles and piles of clothes and shoes and Avon boxes and magazines and tapes of *soaps* and stuff, stuff Black Mama collect: programs from retirement parties, from church events, from weddings, and pictures inside of frames that have pictures taped on top. There ain't enough room, but Black Mama still try to keep it all. Collecting. The house sag and tilt to the side due to the weight of years upon years of dust and other things buried inside those walls. With time, those other things decompose and transform into disappearance. The squeaks of rodents trapped somewhere inside the house, inside the walls, after some days, quiet, and finally turn to silence. She wish the rodents away, but the furry carcass leave a stench, a stench that no incense or Glade spray can cover over. Cain't cover over death, rotting in the walls with nowhere to go, it just linger. And there ain't nothin' Black Mama, Brothers 1 and 2, or Baby Girl can do about it so they all just go through it until, like the squeaks, the scent of dead rodent also be&come

something else, undetectable, disappeared, a ghostly dawdle.

There are so many critters: roaches, mice, spiders, snails ... Baby Girl sometimes bring home worms and lose them inside too. Things get stuck in they house.

When they walk into Black Mama house, they house, they see a pile of shoes, a mountain of years. Decades later, Baby Girl return to they house, and at the bottom of that pile, she find her beat-up Nikes from middle school. She try them on and go for a walk, only to have the soles disintegrate beneath her feet. Black Mama house a collector of whatever land in its arms—whatever *it* is, it don't come to die, but it come to live forever. Living forever, though, can be its own kind of death, as the days get hotter and colder and the dust thicker. Whatever make its way into Black Mama house got little to no chance of leavin'. The fridge, too, packed with food, old food, that never get eaten. There are leftovers, been left over for years, chilled and rotten. Alive and dead all at once.

🦅

Black Mama sit facing the stack of old media machines like old TVs and VCRs that prop the current TV up. The TV sit atop a much older TV, the kind with knobs, dials, and a place for puttin' wire hangers where antennas s'posed to go. Black Mama collect new technologies as they come into

Black Trans Man in his childhood bedroom, 2018.
Photos by Texas Isaiah.

being. Baby Girl remember goin' to Blockbuster to rent videos and a VCR many weekends. The VCRs cased in hard black plastic suitcases. Eventually, Black Mama rent a VCR from the Rent-a-Center. It take about three years to pay it off, and once she do, it break-broke. Money. Lost. Later they get their own VCR, and Black Mama record her stories, *All My Children*. VHS tapes collect themselves like a leaning Jenga tower, unsteady, unstable but never falling. Black Mama sit at the top of the bed, purse turned inside out. Her purse, big and black, always with zippers because "... buttons ain't secure!"

Black Mama carry a big bag and always got at least five cough drops, a few sticks of stale gum, old tissue, a small amount of cash, and a whole host of other things, old things, collected things. Sometimes those things collect their own things, like the cinnamon bears wrapped in cocoons of fuzz. Fuzzy bears never Baby Girl first choice snack, but she don't mind sucking off the fuzz to get to the sweet. Baby Girl love candy, and Black Mama do too.

Black Mama and Baby Girl most of the time eat snacks, Cheez-Its and fruit snacks. Black Mama cook a meal on a Sunday every now and again, but mostly they eat KFC, Church's Chicken, Jack in the Box, and McDonald's but never Taco Bell. Black Mama don't like Taco Bell, something about their meat not really being meat. Black Mama prefer the burrito shop. Baby Girl love burritos too. Black Mama don't like cilantro. Baby Girl don't like it either. Some

Baby Girl and Black Mama celebrating Baby Girl's
birthday at McDonald's, 1988.

things Black Mama do and say, Baby Girl just pick up like
it's her own. She grow up to say "no cilantro" without even
thinking about it. She don't remember when or how Black
Mama dislikes be&come her own. So many other things
be&come a part of Baby Girl desires that ain't her own, she
have to work hard to figure out how to distinguish what she
want and like from what the people she love want and like.
She go through many cycles of losing and finding herself.
Her full shape don't come so easy to her as reflection, even
though she able to see and feel others so well.

Black Mama and Baby Girl go to the burrito shop across the street from *The Center. The Center,* the daycare center, the school where Aunty G is the director and a classroom teacher in the afternoons. They order one super burrito with shredded chicken. Black Mama ask them to cut it in half so she and Baby Girl can share. The burrito so big, they got more than enough. Baby Girl love when Black Mama take them out to places like the burrito shop. She so used to stayin' home with Black Mama 'cause Black Mama don't like to go to too many places, especially without Aunty G. Black Mama like to shop, though. Black Mama love to shop.

Baby Girl love to shop with Black Mama. Baby Girl get to be Black Mama personal stylist. Black Mama always concerned about her own body, she adorn it with care and precision. She always worry too about how big or small she is. When her and Baby Girl walk through the mall, Black Mama ask, "Am I as big as her?" Baby Girl learn the answer always, "No." Baby Girl learn how to say the things Black Mama want to hear. Black Mama favorite place to shop is Mervyn's. Baby Girl enjoy any store where she can play and not get lost. While Black Mama peruse the racks, Baby Girl play. She hide in between sweaters and dresses, twirling and enjoying her retreat into the *Black (w)holeness*[3] of the inner racks. She disappear and sometimes forget about time and Black Mama. At some point, she remember and no longer want to be alone. Sometimes she find Black Mama real quick, but most times it seem like Black

Mama just leave her. Baby Girl start to panic when she cain't find Black Mama. Her ears turn red hot. Her heart beat too fast and too slow at the same time. She start to feel small and shaky-scared. She start to imagine life without Black Mama, and her imagination take her somewhere so dark and lonely, she start to cry. She don't want to be lost no more. She want to be found. The store be&come too big then. But she remember what Black Mama say.

"If you get lost, just turn yourself in."

Baby Girl make her way to the checkout and tell the cashier she lost. Through streams of tears, she gasp, "I'm lost. I cain't find my mama."

"Black Mama, please make your way to aisle number . . ." the voice robotic over the loudspeaker. This happen so often, Baby Girl believe Black Mama secretly tryin' to abandon her. But Black Mama always show up to collect Baby Girl. Baby Girl relieved, and Black Mama act like nothin' happen and kind of laugh. During the time between the page over the loudspeaker and their reunion, Baby Girl already imagine her life as an orphan. The feeling of being forever lost cause her so much anxiety. Black Mama never seem to carry that same worry.

In response to this repeat crisis, Baby Girl develop a keen ear for the clickity-clank of Black Mama keys. She play in the racks of clothing and tune the world out without the fear of be&coming forever lost. There come a point when she get too old to turn herself in to the checkout counter without being laughed at. So her ears be&come a well-honed tool, a tracking device, that always lead her back to Black Mama. Even if Black Mama want to leave without her, Baby Girl know the jingle of those keys. Baby Girl know how to listen. She know Black Mama by the jingle of her keys.

Black Mama lose things sometimes too. Baby Girl walk into Black Mama room, that big black purse turned over and all the things once inside spread all over her full-size mattress. All the things Black Mama carry. One time, Baby Girl walk upstairs to see Black Mama searchin', she searchin' for something. Baby Girl feel the panic in Black Mama and want to help her find whatever it is, but she cain't. Black Mama seem different, but Baby Girl don't quite understand, so she just stand by watchin' Black Mama wrestle with her stuff.

Eventually, Black Mama say, "Come on, we leavin'." Black Mama drive them to Mervyn's and tell Baby Girl she can pick out one thing. Baby Girl pick out two things, and Black Mama buy them both. Baby Girl happy but also feel uneasy. After they leave the store, Black Mama say, "What you want to eat?"

Baby Girl feel brave and say, "Burger King and Chuck E. Cheese!" She wait for Black Mama to say "No!" but Black Mama just keep sayin' "Yes" or "Okay." Baby Girl start to feel more uncomfortable because she so used to Black Mama reminding them that they cain't do everything all the time. Sometimes Black Mama say, "We don't got no McDonald's money!" Or if she really feeling clever when Baby Girl ask for something she cain't afford, she say, "*You* got McDonald's money?" This day seem strange to Baby Girl, and her feelin' wasn't wrong. Somethin' wrong with Black Mama. Later when they get home, Black Mama go upstairs and sit on the bed. This time instead of her purse, she have pills laid out, poured out all 'round her. Baby Girl don't say nothin', she just watch. Black Mama start to cry. Baby Girl watch. Black Mama go downstairs and sit on the toilet, her meditation space. Baby Girl stand beside her, watchin' her sob. She don't know why Black Mama cryin'. Black Mama look at Baby Girl and say, "I'm sorry, Baby Girl. Black Mama gon' die. I cain't live here with you no more." Baby Girl still don't say nothin'. Baby Girl don't even feel too much, she just stuck watchin' and listenin' but not under-standing. Eventually, Black Mama must get tired of Baby Girl bearing witness and tell her to go get Brother 2. Black Mama wear a ring that Daddy buy as an apology for the last time he steal somethin'. Black Mama cain't get the ring off cause her hand done swole up. Her finger suffocate within the confines of the circular hold. Black Mama say, "Go get yo' brother, tell him I'm dyin'."

Baby Girl go outside and find Brother 2 playin'. "Black Mama say come home. She sick. Need help."

Brother 2, Black Mama, and Baby Girl, 1990s.

Brother 2 special. He take things apart and put them back together again, like computers and toilets and stoves. Brother 2 can fix just about anything in the house, so that's why Black Mama want him to come home. He gotta figure out how to get this ring off her swelling finger without cutting the finger off. Brother 2 go next door and borrow a big sharp tool from neighbor and cut the ring off. The ring destroyed. Black Mama finger is free but still swollen and still sore. And she still cryin'. Brother 2 call Aunty G. Aunty G come get Black Mama and take her to the hospital. Black Mama go away for a month. Baby Girl stay with another aunty, Aunty X. No one tell Baby Girl what happen to Black Mama. Aunty X only say, "You cain't stress my sister out, you makin' her sick." Baby Girl immediately feel guilt about asking for two things at Mervyn's and Burger King and Chuck E. Cheese. Baby Girl start to believe she make Black Mama sick. She be&come to believe herself to be Black Mama burden.

They take Baby Girl to visit Black Mama in the hospital, but Baby Girl afraid. She don't want to get close to the bed, she don't want to get close to Black Mama, she don't want to hurt her no more. She don't want to lose Black Mama, and she don't know how to find her either. Black Mama look the same but something different in her eyes. Not just the tears but Baby Girl could tell, Black Mama wasn't Black Mama no more.

Brother 1 and Brother 2 learn early on not to ask Black Mama for everything they want, cause Black Mama do just about anything to get it for them. They Christmases was like nothin' anybody could think to imagine in real life, real Black life, anyways. Black Mama always come home some-time at the end of October with a JCPenny's catalog and say, "Circle what you want." Black Mama never say, "Circle three things, two things, ten things." She just say, "Circle what you want." And the day after Thanksgiving, Black Mama line up three in the morning outside of Mervyn's or Macy's depending on who got the best deals. Black Mama

Brother 2, Baby Girl, and Brother 1 at home, 1980s.

want to give her babies everything they want, she want to fill their wants. She want them to know storybook magic and wonder. As Brother 1 and Brother 2 grow older, they stop askin' Black Mama for *everything* 'cause they start to notice how *everything* cost Black Mama *something*. Brother 1 and Brother 2 are ten and twelve years older than Baby Girl. Baby Girl don't know yet not to ask Black Mama for everything she want.

Brothers' daddy supposed to pay child support of twenty
dollars a month, but he don't. He a present father, though,
and Black Mama grateful for that most times. They daddy
come by on birthdays and leave them gifts, pets: a puppy,
a bird, another bird, or a snake. Black Mama don't like no
animals. Brother 1 and Brother 2 love animals, but in they
house, Black Mama house, it's easy for things to get lost.
One day, Brother 2 lose his snake. Wasn't no luck lookin'
for him, so he just mourn snakey departure. Four months
later, snakey appear in Brother 2 drawer. Black Mama
never know nothing about it. She don't mind if the boys
have pets as long as they keep them safe. Black Mama
not gon' be responsible for the pets. That's her rule, but
of course when something go wrong, and Brother 2 bird
become stiff, and he start to cry, Black Mama say, "Put
birdie in a box, and we'll take him to the hospital." Black
Mama take an hour-long bus ride with Brother 2 and a
dead yellow bird in a shoebox. The whole way she just
trying to hold off on breakin' Brother 2 heart. She want to
give her baby some hope, so they ride together, and when
the vet give them the news that birdie gone, Brother 2
wail. Black Mama catch her breath waiting for the pain
to pass. She really don't like no tears. This why she take
the long ride: She don't want to see her baby cry, and truth
be told, she pray the whole bus ride for a miracle, that
somehow like Jesus, birdie stiff wings might start to flex
once again.

Things get lost. And sometimes lost things cain't be nothing but gone. Like sometime after Black Mama have Brother 2, doctor say, "You done lost your ability to mother again." But Baby Girl come here after. Baby Girl come here a miracle to Black Mama.

Black Mama say it's actually Brother 1 that dream Baby Girl up years before she ever arrive. One day, Black Mama pick Brother 1 up from school, and teacher say, "How's the baby?" Black Mama give Brother 1 a look, and everybody know he in trouble.

"Why you tellin' lies?"

Black Mama believe she cain't have no more babies. She went to Dr. ___. He don't like Black women who have babies, and he don't like Black women who don't want to have they babies. He pretend, though, to be a help to those who come up on some rough times and no longer can bear the weight of carrying. Dr. ___ turn out to be an anti-abortion *activist*. He do over 200 abortive procedures before women start to talk to one another 'bout how Dr. ___ done hurt them *real* bad, so bad they don't want to ever have no more babies or sometimes even be touched at all. Dr. ___ known as the butcher, 'cause "he cut 'em up." Black Mama never question the pain nor the fact that after the procedure, she no longer able to have babies. She believe this how God punish her for refusing to carry like a home supposed to.

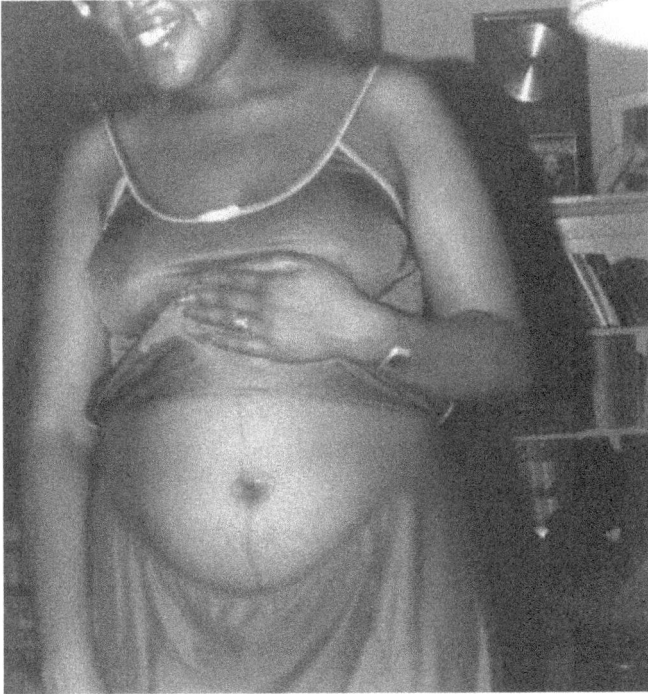

Black Mama carrying Baby Girl, 1984.

Black Mama teach Baby Girl that God is above all things a punisher. God know every wrong, and if they don't confess and somehow die before, they go straight to hell. Baby Girl don't want to go to hell, but even more than that, she just don't like the idea of displeasing God. She want to be good. Baby Girl don't like to displease anyone, especially Black Mama or any teachers at school. Sometimes she don't know why some things bad, just that they bad. Baby Girl come here carrying feelings. But Black Mama also teach Baby Girl how to carry feelings.

Christmas come around, and for Baby Girl, they leave a tree with no gifts in the living room. Black Mama and brothers say, "Baby Girl, you sleep, and Santa will come." Baby Girl sleep but wake up every hour askin' Black Mama if Santa come yet. Black Mama hush her back to sleep. At some point in the wee hours of the morning, brothers and Black Mama go downstairs, and in all the hiding places in their house, they pull out black garbage bags filled with gifts, gifts from Black Mama, but sometimes Black Mama write on the gift tag, *from Santa* or *from Daddy*. The gifts unloaded, and there is no order, they create a mountain of gifts that surround the tree. Baby Girl can barely see the top third of the tree after Santa come. Black Mama want to give her babies joy and surprise. Baby Girl always have the most gifts, and no one ever question this: She baby and she a girl, she special. Baby Girl don't know why, but she start to believe too that she special. Baby Girl believe she have a superpower of being connected to Jesus, and for Baby Girl, it's not just a belief, it's the truth.

The truth is, miracles happen, and if Black Mama and Baby Girl pray hard enough, long enough, believe enough, they can change reality. Black Mama try to change reality during Christmas by making her babies feel like royalty, she spoil them. She is too overcompensating for what had been occurring in her life. Baby Girl Daddy, who no longer in prison, he home, and he make home heavy with his moods and all his stealing. He take anything and everything. He on crack. Before Christmas, Daddy disappear for a few weeks, then show up the morning of, just in time for gifts, and Black Mama got his already labeled and ready underneath the tree. Daddy say he don't want to go to the big family dinner after they open gifts. Black Mama say he cain't stay at the house while they gone, so he leave. They all leave the house. When they get back home, window broken. And Daddy done took Christmas. There's only scraps of wrapping paper trickled around the tree where the heap of gifts once rested. Black Mama too through but not ever really done with lovin' Daddy. To make that Christmas happen, Black Mama take on a part-time job at a department store on top of her everyday social workin'. She exhausted and all that she work for, gone . . . lost. Black Mama cain't breathe. Black Mama cain't hold her breath no more. She cain't inhale, and she cain't exhale. Alive and dead at the same time. Black Mama be&come lost beneath the covers of her bed in dark silence.

Black Mama still believe in love and God and Jesus and faith. Black Mama tell Baby Girl, "If you pray, your prayers can bring Daddy home. You can save him." And Baby Girl believe that she can save people, something she have to unbe&uncome, a savior complex. Brother 2 say, "Yo' daddy take everything. Yo' daddy take. My daddy bring gifts. Yo' daddy on drugs. My daddy just a liar like normal daddies. You look just like yo' daddy, like he done spit you out." Baby Girl belly feel heavy with the weight of carrying Daddy

Black Mama, Brother 1, and Baby Girl on the front porch, 1980s.

deeds. And she hate the feeling of being made of Daddy
spit since his breath always smell like stale beer. Baby Girl
imagine herself a cloud of stale ale, and she don't like it. She
don't want Daddy face on her, but everyone keep reminding
her of what she carry that she got no choice over. She look
in the mirror and see the face of the man who steal Christmas. She lost, don't know how to not feel responsible for all
the things Daddy do. She vow to stay by Black Mama and
take care of what Daddy neglect. Baby Girl can sense, Black

Mama, too, come here carrying feelings, mostly people just say she crazy though, say sometimes she just lose it, and it's not all right. They call her schizophrenic, bipolar, a breakdown in nervousness, but Baby Girl always call her home. She always know how to find Black Mama by the distinct jingle of her keys, a chime sound that make be&coming lost not so scary anymore.

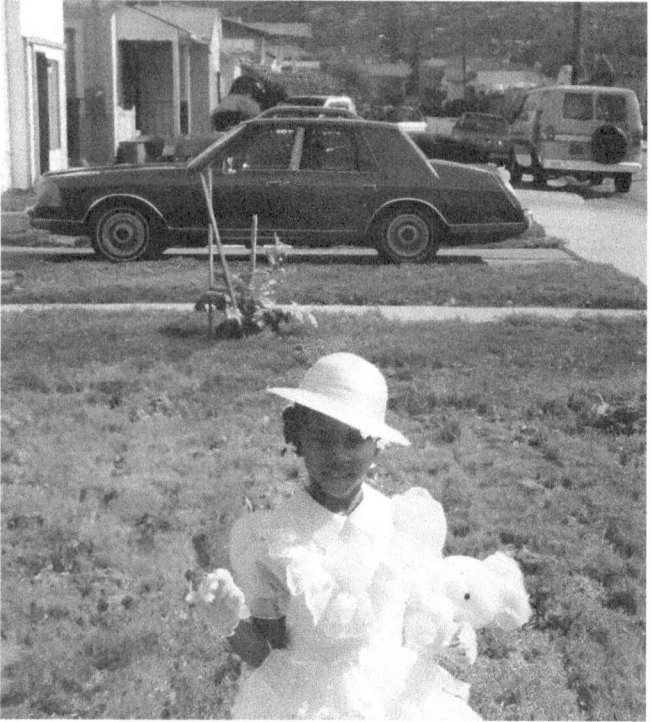

Baby Girl poses on the front lawn before
Easter church service, 1980s.

CHAPTER 3

Special

Special [Adjective]: *better, greater, or otherwise differ-ent from what is usual.*[1]

Queer. strange. odd. *funny like that.*

Baby Girl deemed *special* from the time she wake Black Mama up. She wrangle all her strength to get back to this place called Earth. Later in life, when Baby Girl no longer Baby Girl, they will visit a seer who tells a tale of Black Mama and Baby Girl tethered together for multiple life-times. Baby Girl come to protect Black Mama, but perhaps this lifetime Baby Girl have to make a new relationship to herself and a new relationship to Black Mama. Perhaps this journey to Earth, this time, be one of reckoning with God and the Ancestors she long to be loved and held by.

Black Mama in the bathroom sweatin', body achin', some-thin' wrong. She feel it, she know it, she gon' die. That's what she thinking. She make the call that she won't be going into work and take herself to the hospital dreading the news she'll surely have to give to brothers later that day. When the doctor return with news of a new arrival,

Black Mama say, "No, this just cain't be. The doctor told me . . ." And she drift off to the memory of the day they get the news that Black Mama cain't carry:

"Tell him, I want him to know."

Black Mama and Daddy sit in front the doctor as he explain, "Black Mama is no longer able to bear children." Black Mama carry shame because Daddy is childless, but she got two sons. She feel guilty that she cain't bear, for him, a child. Daddy don't care; he love Black Mama and ain't so sure about children anyway.

She drift back to the present, and as the reality sink in that she is indeed pregnant, she sit there realizing how alone she is. Daddy dreamin' done got him locked up again. She already got two boys, and now Baby Girl done unsettled her belly too. Immediately, Black Mama call Aunty G, and Aunty G is nothing but glad ". . . that Baby Girl is gon' be Aunty G Baby Girl." But it's still true that Daddy locked up, and Black Mama feel alone. Daddy won't be out in time for delivery.

Black Mama stand up and decidedly exit the doctor's office making her way to work, angry that she take a day off for something as trivial as pregnancy.

Daddy have no babies. Black Mama want to give him the gift of fatherhood. She believe a little one of his own might be the miracle to save him from the streets, the thieving and the druggin'. He a binge user so there are times when

Black Daddy and Baby Girl, 1987.

he is present and weeks, sometimes months, when he just
disappear into the landscape of Oakland's secret streets.

After Baby Girl born: When Daddy around, he take Baby
Girl with him everywhere. He take her to his rehearsals,
where he play the bass guitar and sing soprano with local
gospel doo-wop groups. Daddy can sing all the parts if

needed. When Daddy home and sober, he a classic man, doting over his waves and the way his suits cling to his body just right. He teach Baby Girl how to look in the mirror. He a stickler about ironing his clothes and having the perfect crease in his pants. Once, he take Baby Girl for a walk to all his spots, spots he warn that she never visit alone. He take her to a world behind the train tracks where people set up tents and the ground littered with trash. It's a world that Baby Girl and Black Mama drive over and past daily, but Black Mama never take those walks. Daddy want Baby Girl to know the world outside of Black Mama car.

Baby Girl remember the walks they take down East 14th, it's where he teach her how to pee standing up. Daddy know everyone. He got friends in those streets, street people, people Baby Girl and Black Mama ignore when they driving, people Black Mama never talk to. The first transgender person Baby Girl recall meeting is on a walk with Daddy. They walk to the store, and at the bus stop on the corner, a dark trans woman sit on the bench. Baby Girl already staring even before they reach her. She would have continued to stare and walk on by, but Daddy greet her like he do everyone else on that street, with smiles and an upbeat "What's happenin'?" Baby Girl afraid. She cain't see the full humanity of that woman at the bus stop. She grab Daddy hand, hoping to signal her discomfort. Daddy hold her hand and take a step back. He look at Baby Girl and compassionately whisper, "It's okay. I have all kinds of friends, and that's okay."

Baby Girl be&come Daddy's Girl until she ain't. There come a time when Baby Girl start to despise those people on the street because she know those the people Daddy with when he not with them. Black Mama tell Baby Girl to pray for Daddy.

🐦

Daddy been gone for over three weeks, and Black Mama stressed in searchin'. She call to see if maybe he get locked up again, even pray that he get locked up so at least they know where he at.

Black Mama say to Baby Girl, "If you pray, your prayers can bring Daddy home."

Black Mama and Baby Girl go searching for Daddy in those places Black Mama never go, those places Daddy warn Baby Girl to never go alone. They find him huddled up in a group of houseless people in an abandoned lot. He there, and they driving by. Black Mama stop, and Daddy come over and ask for some money. He come home eventually.

The filth he carry back home in sullen clothes make Baby Girl cringe. He s'posed to be beautiful, the handsome meticulous man in the mirror. But he come home carrying nothin' but himself and the outdoors. Black Mama stand by smoking while he clean himself up a little. Every time he come home from one of his binges, it's a whole-day affair of apologies and *I wishes.* Sometimes Baby Girl

act as mediator between Black Mama and Daddy, askin',
". . . and how do that make you feel?" Daddy comin' home
always the same and always different. He know how to cry.
He know how to ask for forgiveness like it's the first and
last time. But Daddy move in cycles of his own time and his
own making. He move back home, giving the feeling of a
small trickle of faucet water gently caressing the palm of
your hand, but that trickle never stay trickle, it be&come
full flow and then overflow in outbursts. Sometimes he
don't even say sorry, just come home, mad after weeks of
being away and not callin'. He come home mad 'cause the
thrill done gone, and all he have to come back to is Black
Mama and Baby Girl. He miss the moon and the stars high.
Sometimes, though, when Daddy home long enough to
remember all the love they got for him, he become as sweet
as molasses and as cool as Michael Jackson's red leather
jacket. He take Baby Girl and Black Mama out for dreamin'.
They share their dreams for Baby Girl, that one day she
might be&come bright as the sun. They know she gon' be
special because she ain't supposed to be in the first place.

🐦

Before Baby Girl born: The Sunday just before Daddy got
locked up again, Black Mama hold Daddy hand tight while
the preacher speak of miracles and how "Jesus be on the
main line TODAY!" Preacher make it seem like *this* Sunday
is something special, enunciating T-O-D-A-Y like a huge red
tag sale at some department store. Just as quickly as Black
Mama hold on to Husband hand, she let it go and reach for

her Bible snuggled in the back of the maroon pew. She pick up a note card from her Bible and jot:

Dear God, bless me with a baby.
Dear God, make my husband whole.
Dear God, bless our union.
Dear God, give us favor.
Dear God, Let us rest in faith.

Black Mama be made of dreams too.

When Black Mama walk out of service, she drop that slip of paper into the prayer box.

Daddy silent that day. No one really know what he dreamin' about.

Black Mama dream up her miracle baby finally. She gon' finally have herself a Baby Girl to love. Someone with a heart like her own. She love her boys, but there's something special about a daughter, something she believe they can share that the boys cain't.

She prepare her home for Baby Girl, buying Cabbage Patch dolls that Brother 2 eventually cut up because "Nobody ask me if I want a sister anyway." Brother 2 don't want a sister, he want to be the baby. But there ain't no stoppin' Black Mama and Daddy miracle. Black Mama never angry about her miracle baby despite the circumstances.

Daddy get locked up right after they get the news. He get scared and try to rob his way to financial security. Daddy

Baby Girl holding her Cabbage Patch dolls
and eating a cookie, 1980s.

ain't a great thief, but that don't keep him from tryin'. When
he twelve, he run a whole group of young robbers, including his number one fan, his little sister, Lil. One time, Daddy
and Lil run away to Los Angeles. They hitchhike all the way
there from Oakland and go for broke on some random LA
streets. Lil was little, too little to ride with the big boys, so
they drop her off at a random school for girls, orphans. No
one ever talk about what happen at that school. Just one
day, Lil come back home changed.

Black Mama remember all the stories Daddy tell her about his robbing schemes. They excite her. He don't lie to her. He tell her he *used* to be, but he done be&come something else 'cause God done changed him. He lie to her. He tell Black Mama a dream, and she search to live there and hold that vision down or up while he away. She prepare a home for Baby Girl. Buy clothes. Buy a crib. Buy it all. Still working. Still poor.

As the pregnancy continue, Black Mama become less and less able to hold herself and Baby Girl. The doctor place her on bed rest 'cause Baby Girl just too long, too much limb for Black Mama body, too much pressure.

Baby Girl never an easy child to carry or hold on to. She special. She always doin' somethin' different. She always hurtin' herself playin' outside. Last time she go to the doctor for another broken ankle, the doctors ask Black Mama if they can talk to Baby Girl alone. Black Mama agree. They ask Baby Girl, "What really happened?" And she respond, "I fell down again. I really did." Baby Girl a funny girl. She silly. She awkward. She clumsy. She fall down a lot but always get back up again, no tears, no cryin'. She get used to the pain of the fall, even the ones that cause broken bones, but she know when it's broken always. Black Mama warn there better really be something wrong if she gotta take off work to take babies to the doctor or the emergency room. Baby Girl more afraid of what Black Mama might do if nothin' wrong than the consequences of actually being hurt. She pray it's broken again.

Baby Girl family big on both sides, though she spend most of her time with Black Mama side. They love games, singing, drinking coffee, and telling stories. Baby Girl got over twenty cousins and most of them raised to be more like siblings, meaning there's a closeness there, especially with Aunty G and her kids. Aunty G always take in more than just her own children, there come a time when Brother 1 and Brother 2 live with Aunty G too. The cousins band together, and it's Baby Girl favorite place to be, going to Aunty G house after church or on some random Saturday night.

Cuzzy. Cuzzy. Cuzzy Corporation. is the slogan they sing to call themselves into legitimacy, a power bloc in the family, the band of cousins. Baby Girl love being with cousins, every time someone get in trouble, someone get angry and start a fight on the basketball court, and the talent shows where everyone got to participate. Once, Cousin C get a whoopin' for refusing to perform.

The cousins all each other's best friends, ride or dies. They shoot dice upstairs, where folk bring out socks filled with coins for making bets. Side deals made before the game: "I'll loan you four quarters for five percent . . ." Baby Girl never learn how to shoot dice, but she love to watch and be

Aunty G and Black Mama perform at a Christmas talent show, 2011.

a part of the action as jokes fly back and forth from cousin to cousin, big and small. Baby Girl have a gap, and one cousin go in on the spaciousness of her teeth, and she laugh too because it's funny. They laugh a lot in they family. Laughter be&come medicine for the tough realities. They practice be&coming tough in they family. Black Mama and siblings recall how they daddy, Granddaddy, make the girls fight the boys, brothers against sisters so the girls know how to protect themselves. Nobody ever talk about what lesson the boys supposed to learn. But they tell the story with pride again and again. Black Mama and aunties be&come strong women, but Aunty G the most fearless of them all.

Baby Girl and a small group of cousins hang out at Aunty N's house. Uncle M, Aunty N husband, who Baby Girl hate because he always be *the tickle monster*, tickle her, and it's unlike anything she feel before. She laugh, but she don't want to be laughin'. She want to say "Stop!" but cain't disrupt the laughter flowing from her body. It take her some time, but she eventually learn how to make him stop. She learn how not to respond to his tickling fingers. If she don't respond, if she can bear Uncle M touch without any laughter, then the game no longer fun for him. She proud of herself for learning how to not feel. An early learned practice of dissociation. She learn to make herself numb when she want to be. She take control of her body.

While they at Aunty N's one day, Uncle M all of a sudden jump up and out toward Cousin C and place her in a chokehold. Baby Girl and all cousins run up on Uncle M. Some cousins start crying or at least they eyes red in rage fightin' tears. Cousin C just look scared-shocked. Everything move in slow motion for Baby Girl. She calm. She don't cry. Black Mama don't like no tears.

Cousins and Baby Girl leave Aunty N house and call Aunty G. She meet them back at her house, all the cousins and they friends, some of whom now stay with Aunty G too. They be&come cousins too, eligible to join the *Cuzzy. Cuzzy. Cuzzy Corporation.* Aunty G take care of everybody, she cain't really cook too good. But Aunty G an OG, a superhero in Baby Girl eyes. When she get to the house, she line all the cousins up in a horizontal line facing her. It's mostly silent, but there's still some sobby-snifflin'. Baby Girl just stand attention and watch, wonderin' if they in trouble. She wonderin' why Uncle M come after Cousin C in the first place. Why would a grown man do that to a teenager and, of all people, Cousin C? She nerdy. She can be mean, but she don't really bother nobody. She spend most her time in libraries reading books and winning competitions for reading the most books in a month. Aunty G look at cousins and, with all seriousness, walk past each one of them like a sergeant. She give a speech that galvanize cousins like a coach talkin' to a basketball team that got fifteen seconds to break the tie before the game over. She prepare cousins like little warriors. "Anytime anyone come up on your family like that, you need to be prepared to fight! Now take a look in the room around you—if you had to fight right now, what could you use as a weapon?"

Baby Girl blurt out, "Bleach!"

Aunty G respond, "Bleach! Okay, so what you gon' do with that?"

Baby Girl say, "Throw it in his face!"

"Okay, good, what else!?" Aunty G move on as they go through a list of possible weapons. Then Aunty G demonstrate for everybody how to get out a chokehold. Aunty G a warrior type, but Black Mama live by the *turn the other cheek* model, even though she can get loud and yell anyone out of a room. Although Baby Girl fascinated by being part of Aunty G army, when she alone, she practice Black Mama *turn the other cheek* model. This cause her to get bullied a lot, especially since she always askin' people to take Jesus into they hearts. Most her friends in elementary school Jehovah's Witnesses. They the only kids that understand the love and fear of God as much as Baby Girl do.

Laughter is medicine for the tough realities of what it's like when Baby Girl have to go back home with Black Mama to Daddy depression and cold. Baby Girl fantasize about the next talent show. The singing and the shouting, the Holy Ghost dancin' competitions. Baby Girl family competitive and always up to learn a new game. They drink coffee like cocktails, sampling different kinds of flavored creamer. Baby Girl start drinking coffee when she five, and it don't stunt her growth.

She gon' grow and be&come. She already be&come so in love with love. Her capacity for love is great, something she learn from Black Mama side of the family. She stay up all night recording love songs from the radio to a tape. She wrap it up and give it to SB, a boy she like in her class. He bring the tape back to her the next day and say, "My mama say I cain't have this." She hurt feelins but move on to a new crush. She always got a crush, always playin' house and dreamin' of her future love story with a mama, daddy, and some babies. Relationships in elementary school don't last long, and the relationships Baby Girl witness in her family don't seem to ever end.

Her family never use the words polyamory or nonmonogamy, but they live and love queerly in that way, naturally. There never a time when Baby Girl don't remember her family and how it grow every time someone get divorced and then remarry. At Granny funeral, they remember Uncle B third ex-wife comin' up to them and proudly introducing herself, "Hi, I don't know if you remember me, but I'm Uncle B third wife." All the women in the family at the funeral get to choose one of Granny church hats to wear in honor of Granny. It don't matter if they ex or current wife, they still get to choose a hat. Baby Girl don't get no hat 'cause by that time she be&come Black Trans Man. Black Trans Man look around the sanctuary and notice how packed it is. They start seating people in the choir pews behind the pulpit. And that's when he look over to brothers and say, "Look! Yo' daddy here too!"

They don't say goodbye in they family. Christmas breakfast most years happen at Uncle A house, one of Aunty G's ex-husbands. They got five children together, and every Christmas, the family all go to Uncle A and Miss B house. Miss B and Uncle A also got two children. They all a big family. Aunty G ex-husband and new husband get along fine too, be&come family too. They never let anyone go, everyone still welcome even after the messiest of divorces. Someone's ex bound to show up, not just her, but her new husband, their baby, his kids, and her mama. And everyone kind and welcoming. There only a few whispers of "Wow! She just brought her *whole* family!" They whisper like they don't know that's what happens every year, just like every year, they know that Cousin R gon' show up with her husband and all her kids and never bring a dish to share at family potlucks. They know she only start coming to family events when it's getting close to the time of her children's birthdays, and though people say things and feel some kind of way, they all show up for the babies' birthday parties because they family.

They stick together. They don't let anyone from outside come in and harm family, even if they harm one another. Black Mama and Aunty G talk about how Granddaddy believe in family, strong family, they protect one another. They say, when they was kids, if they ever run from a fight or leave one of they siblings to fight alone, Granddaddy beat them.

Aunty G never really get whoopins though, she too sensitive, always a performer. When asked to go pick a switch, she come back with the tiniest of twigs, and for that, she get in more trouble. In the retelling, Aunty G always say, "Now, why in the world would I ever go grab a big stick? For my own whoopin'?! I'm not crazy!" and then everyone bust out laughin'.

Baby Girl and most all her cousins graduates of 24 Hour Children Center, *The Center*. Baby Girl and other cousins who go on to college are also recipients of a scholarship from one of Aunty G's other endeavors. Aunty G work not only to make a better community for Black women in particular, but she also work hard so that her people, the ones around her, have access to something better. Aunty G ain't never scared. She always keep a bat in the trunk of her car. Aunty G the reason why Baby Girl don't sit with her back turned to the door in public space, she always wanna know what's goin' on. She look out for danger, and she calm when it come. She and they whole family special. better. greater. or otherwise different from what is usual. queer. strange. odd. *funny like that.*

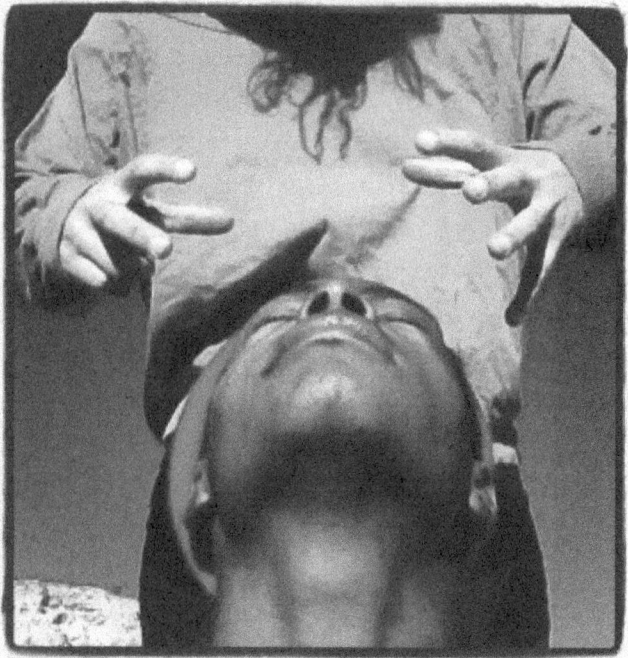

Black Trans Man and Anna Martine Whitehead
in Joshua Tree, 2010s.

CHAPTER 4

Hands

Hands [Plural noun]: *Hands can be so soft and sweet like the smoothest of rose petals.* Hands can be coarse and dry, hitting the skin rough-tough like the thorns of rose stems. Hands can hold like the prickly stems protect the delicate petals. Hands can be held—tight—sweat between palms in the touching. Hands can be hard and harsh in the whippin' of little children. Hands can be sharp, stinging behinds, and pants-down . . .

"She's a switch mama!" or "He's a switch daddy!" Make you go out to the yard and pluck the switch for your own beating. Daddy run away from the beatin' of hands upon his body. Baby Girl only imagine what Black Mama did because she don't ever say, just nod and agree with Aunty G.

Aunty G say, "Must be crazy to think I'mma pick the biggest switch for my own beatin' of body . . . Hell, no!"

And Grandma's hands, Daddy mama, her hands soften over time. But they could be brutal . . . same hands make gumbo out this world full of Louisiana lovin', same hands that take that belt across a Daddy side cousin bare bottom. Baby Girl only bear witness by peeking in the crack of the partially closed door, she cain't see cousin face, just her bottom and Grandma belt a lashin'. Baby Girl cain't remember a whimper, a holler, or even silence, but she feel her cousin cryin'—a stuttering low murmur of "I'm hurtin', your hands is a hurtin' on me!"

BABY GIRL HANDS

Baby Girl come out the womb touchin' her private parts, a habit no prayer can exorcise. Black Mama and Aunty G and everybody be&come full of shame with Baby Girl touchin' herself like that.

Must be somebody touching her.

But there ain't nobody touchin' Baby Girl, not then, not when she was a baby and a toddler. Her body then only hers for the touchin'. As she grow, she learn that the touchin' of oneself not of God. She pray for both forgiveness and deliverance. But she cain't overcome the touch of herself against herself.

She fast. She fast. She tryin' to be grown. Nobody ever say, "She just baby being baby." They make her, right then, a girl, a girl who gon' carry they shame, a girlhood shame. A shame that tell her it's a grotesque act to touch oneself, love oneself, and be okay, even proud of the ability to self soothe.

Baby Girl write letters to God:

Dear God,
If I do it again, kill me.
Love, Baby Girl

She cain't stop, and she keep on livin' while hidin' the pleasure of her own hand upon her own body—her *own* body.

Her hands ain't pure. She believe what preacher preach and how once Black Mama say, "I rather you have sex than touch yo'self like that."

Baby Girl don't know what sex is until kindergarten when a classmate go around the room saying the word "sex." He sometimes sit behind kids and tickle them inside their pants. He do that to Baby Girl once, and she don't dislike it but know it's wrong. They kids, but maybe someone is touchin' this baby—maybe. He share his touch with the class, and Baby Girl go home and ask Black Mama straight out, "What is sex?" Black Mama don't answer the question, only ask, "Where you hear that from?" Baby Girl can tell by Black Mama tone that there's more in the question, somethin' Baby Girl think she'll get in trouble for but not really knowin' why. This seem big, and Black Mama preoccupied by how Baby Girl learn this new term, sex. She afraid someone touchin' her baby. It happens to plenty a baby girls, almost all the girls in Baby Girl family, though they may not talk about it or even view it as a time when hands used in nonconsensual touch because of age, rage, or something else, something else Baby Girl don't really understand.

Baby Girl be&come afraid of touch, especially down there. It mean sin. It mean danger. It's not really hers for the touching. It's special. It's private. It's her coochie. Kit Kat. Kitty kat. Down there. Them parts. The naming make Baby Girl uncomfortable. Why name this thing that's always so close to sin? Why not keep it hidden and unspoken like pleasure for Baby Girl? Baby Girl start to fear what her body can do on its own, and that fear, coupled with shame and guilt, make Baby Girl feel alienated from body be&coming.

DADDY HANDS

He play a lonely baritone tone
A "Night and Day"[1] Daddy
He live for the high to the moon
In the afternoon
She watch. she listen. she learn.
She dream his song grand and gon' save her
Maybe not, but she learn to play something still.
Only one scale she know
But she play it like it's the only one that's ever been written
Blues.
12 bars that's all she need
12 bars that's what he play and hand down to she
No way she reject it
Because he sell everything else for the riff of a lifetime that
    never last
And it never replay itself quite like the first time it play

Addicted to the feeling of the sound, he pay his blues
And what's left is his gift to the world
These strings and their hands
His guitar, the only thing he never sell
His blues
Hers to play now.
She cain't refuse it
Because in his voice, she hear a cry, a plea
Without saying it, his blues his apology to she
And though most people want to inherit the world
She satisfied with strings that cry.
He walk away, and she know he won't be back
He have to catch the train
She want to stop him but never do
Some highs so good they just cain't be understood
But she always do understand.
She look for it too
She start to play that song on that guitar
But silence—
It's broke.
And in that quiet, there's no blue note more true
This blue,
He teach it to her in dark basement afternoons, between
    gin and juice
Somewhere between the sweet in the bitter, clamoring shouts
    and deafening silences
Yes, somewhere between stars and dust
They always know
The blues, and it ain't that bad.

Daddy hands lash out without ever layin' a finger on the body. It's in the way he say goodbye. Or perhaps the way he say hello, like he gon' stay a little while longer. Daddy hands write the most beautiful cursive letters, they look like music notes. He use his hands to make up songs. A soundtrack to his life—fast and hard, romantic and humorous, and sometimes dark, hiding under the blankets for weeks, lonely and melancholic. Daddy hands also so sweet, givin' gifts of gold earrings and chains to Black Mama and Baby Girl. Daddy got the hands of a thief—stealing gold earrings and chains back when he need another fix.

Daddy cook like no other daddy. He also do Baby Girl hair better than most mamas. When Daddy home, he use his hands to cook and do hair and help Black Mama keep the house together—when he sober. When he not sober, his hands used for lyin', takin', and collect calls. He on a binge again, and his hands just disappear. They reappear sometimes, ghostly. Baby Girl and Black Mama go out lookin' for Daddy after he gone for three weeks. Come home one day to window smashed by brick. Daddy climb in and take whatever he can carry. That's why Black Mama start to keep an always-locked room. That's why Black Mama start sleepin' with her purse underneath her head. She tell Baby Girl to keep this secret. Daddy hands leave scars without ever touching the body. Daddy write love in letters that touch something beyond the body. Daddy known less through touchin' and more through feelin'.

MAMA HANDS

Black Mama like to do hair, but she ain't very good at the stylin' part. She put so much time into doin' Baby Girl hair. Baby Girl sit in between Black Mama warm thighs as she meticulously part, scratch, grease, and press each section of Baby Girl hair. It's rare Baby Girl get burned by the hot comb because Black Mama so careful. "Hold you ear back now," she warn. There's some mishaps, of course, but Black Mama think Baby Girl hair precious, and she want it to grow long.

After that summer (she eight), Baby Girl hair fall out from the middle—some kind of growth that doctors cain't explain. Black Mama do all she can to bring her baby hair back. She use all kinds of shampoos and balms— Glover's Mane, Sulfur8, coconut mango grease—but none of them get rid of the gaping scab right in the middle of Baby Girl head, just spreadin' out towards the edges. Brother 2 remind Baby Girl that not only do she got a huge scab on her head, but it smell like somethin' rotting. She don't laugh at his jokes. Doctor say she ain't gon' ever grow hair again. Black Mama pray to God, "Please heal my Baby Girl!" It grow again but never the same. She got a soft spot in the middle where the infection first start workin' its way out from the center. That center patch remain thin, tender, deli-cate, a place that Baby Girl only come to share with lovers.

Black Mama cain't do hair like Daddy. She cain't cook like Daddy, but she bake pineapple coconut cake, sweet potato pies, and make sweet breakfast rice and Malt-o-Meal. Black Mama make everything sweet, and Baby Girl love the sweet of Black Mama sugar. Black Mama drive Baby Girl to the Gingerbread House in downtown Oakland just so they can admire the outside of this life-sized gingerbread house. They never go inside because Black Mama say it's too expensive and "We don't got Gingerbread House money." Baby Girl love the admirin', and she imagine eatin' the whole house with Black Mama, laughin' as they take in the delightful sweetness of the rooftop, the walls, and the stairs.

Black Mama hands strong but over time become weak—so weak. Her right hand so much so that she have to learn how to use her left for writing, driving, and being. Her right arm "constantly on fire," she say. She walk around with her right hand wrapped up in one of Baby Girl wrist guards, which Baby Girl think odd because she break her wrist while wearin' that same wrist guard. After Black Mama wrap her hand, she put the whole thing in a plastic shopping bag filled with ice. She walk around in the heat of a California summer with a long black leather jacket, wrapped hand in shopping bag that start to drip water as the ice melt. Black Mama smell like menthol, Tiger Balm, and Icy Hot—she try it all. One time the salve on Black Mama hands seep into one of her sweet potato pies. They laugh about it in the future, but right then it's just a reminder of Black Mama being unwell again.

Baby Girl embarrassed to go out with Black Mama

when she like this. Baby Girl don't think about the pain Black Mama really feelin', a pain on the inside that cause a fire on the outside. Black Mama be&come frustrated with her body and its inability to move how it used to move. She have to adjust and the adjustin' is a hurtin', a recognition of disability. She fight against it, being labeled a disability. Black Mama take medical leave from work, and that crush her. Push her into a heavy, long depression and a feelin' of worthlessness. It's too much to hold, so it end with another break. break. breakin' . . . She be&come angry-loud.

Black Mama yell. She shout. She wake Baby Girl up before sunrise, screamin', "Take out the trash! Where is my ___? Can you fix the computer?" Black Mama up before the sun, gettin' ready, gettin' ready to get Baby Girl ready. Black Mama join a gym and get Baby Girl a pass too. Before the yellin' and when Black Mama still workin', they wake up 4:30 in the morning to work out. They both like the jacuzzi the most. Baby Girl watch Black Mama as the bubbles from the jacuzzi brush against her brown skin. Black Mama sit, head tilted back, just breathin'—full inhales and exhales. Then they leave and get ready for work and school. The gym a break for Black Mama. She sneak it in in the wee hours of the mornin'. Black Mama stop time to temporarily be&come peace-quiet-calm. And Baby Girl bask in Black Mama peace-quiet-calm until it be&come something else, angry-loud-outlandish. Black Mama break. Baby Girl stay woke, ready to tend to Black Mama in the breakin', though she too need a break sometimes.

GRANDMA HANDS

Grandma hands, Daddy mama hands, never touch Baby Girl in a hurtin' kinda way on account of the first time she try to reach out her hand to slap Baby Girl hand to discipline her. Baby Girl cain't resist stickin' her small thin fingers into the holes of Grandma lace tablecloth that cover the plastic underneath, protection for the glass table beneath it. Grandma tell Baby Girl to cut it out, but Baby Girl continue stretching out the tiny holes. Grandma take her hand and tap Baby Girl. It was a small sting, but it stung, and Baby Girl start to just a hoop-n-holler. Daddy get mad, fire mad. He snatch Baby Girl from her chair and carry her straight out the door screamin', "You ain't gon' ever see her again!"

Grandma call Black Mama just to say, "It wasn't nothin' but a little tap," and "I got a right to discipline my grandbabies."

Daddy say, "No! Never!"

It's said that many of Grandma's boyfriends, husbands, and ex-husbands beat on Daddy bad. Daddy don't accept that for Baby Girl. The baby everybody say he spit out, 'cause she look just like him. Baby Girl his baby but also his friend. He love to play and walk the town with her. He like to show her off. He don't want nothin' to hurt her, and he gon' protect her from pain if he can. Grandma whippin' hands, Daddy demand, "bet' not touch Baby Girl like that again!" It ain't the same for other cousins on Daddy side, though. They get beat. But Grandma hands much

84

more than a hurtin'-beatin'. She why Daddy know how to cook so good. It's Grandma gumbo recipe that get passed around, no written instructions, just some basic ingredients spoken over the phone, then the inheritor have to figure out the rest on they own. Baby Girl stumble upon the right recipe one day. She slow cook and taste test her way back to Grandma gumbo long after Grandma pass away, and she feel Grandma warm-cozy-clean in that pot of stewing gumbo. Nobody do it like Grandma, not even Daddy, though he get close.

Baby Girl spend most mornings and afternoons at Grandma house with cousins who Grandma take care of. Grandma address is the one Black Mama use for her to be able to go to a better school than the one in her neighborhood. At Grandma house, there are only two reasons they gather round her bed, most times it's to pray. Every morning, Grandma, Big Daddy, Grandma's husband, Baby Girl, and whichever one of Baby Girl's cousins there have to pray out loud. Baby Girl always nervous when it come time for her to pray, she wonder if cousins feel the same but never ask. The other time someone gather 'round Grandma bed is for a whoopin.' She make cousins bend over, pants down, and use a leather belt made for a lastin' lashin'. Baby Girl peek through the cracked door but say and do nothin' except hold it. After the whoopin', she don't know what to say to cousins. It don't seem like a time for playin'. She pray for time to move along swiftly so she can be somewhere else, somewhere in Grandma gossip and laughter.

Grandma love to talk. She touch people with her talkin'. Black Mama say, "Come right outside when I get there to pick you up, 'cause I cain't talk with Grandma today." Sometimes Baby Girl forget to come right out, and sometimes she just pretend to forget 'cause she like hearin' Grandma and Black Mama talk. Grandma talk for hours. She talk about anything and everything: suspicions of Whitney Houston *being that way, kinda funny-like*, the trials of OJ Simpson, somebody's baby, food, the Bible, her Bible study classes, and the list go on. She love to talk, it fill her up. Baby Girl and Brother 2 grow up to be talkers too. Baby Girl and Grandma talk to each other a lot. Grandma Baby Girl first audience, she always got time for Baby Girl performances. Sometimes it's just Baby Girl, and other times Baby Girl organize cousins into a singing group; she the leader. Grandma pause her TV shows or turn them all the way down so she can focus on Baby Girl makin'. Baby Girl bring her thirty-key keyboard and play three notes, *dun dun dun, dun dun dun, dundun dun dun dun*. Baby Girl love to see Grandma smile and laugh.

One night after Grandma go to bed, Baby Girl and cousins decide to play in the dark. Candy man in the bathroom mirror. They just runnin' around in the dark. Baby Girl trip over somethin', and a lamp fall down. It don't break, but it's loud. Everybody get in trouble except for Baby Girl. Cousins don't ever get mad at Baby Girl, and they don't talk about the whippins. It's just somethin' they come to accept as part of being kids. Daddy declaration that Baby Girl ain't gon' be subject to Grandma beatins speak to the way he love and try to protect Baby Girl. Daddy touch gentle, Baby Girl body never unsafe when in Daddy care, even when Daddy take her to back-alley blues night pimpin' in the back, babies playin' in the other room, gin and juice gulpin', sour pop and hot crack rock. Her body never experience unsolicited touch when Daddy around.

Grandma hands full with grief. All her babies *on that stuff.* And no matter how much prayin' she do, they always backslide into street life. Grandma always a home for her babies to return to still. That's where Daddy go to live every time Black Mama kick him out. Grandma move out of Oakland to Stockton, and all her babies follow. Grandma hold home safe so they always got a place to come back to. Grandma hands hold.

COUSIN HANDS

Baby Girl remember the first time she look at herself and think, *I'm a cute boy.* She eight, and Cousin X thirteen. She eight, and Cousin X cool. She dark brown, and Cousin X light bright. They stand in the mirror together and imagine themselves as the hip-hop duo Kris Kross. Baby Girl think she look good, Cousin X think she look better. Baby Girl in second grade, Cousin X in middle school. Black Mama home from the hospital, but she need more rest. So Baby Girl stay with Aunty X for the summer. Cousin X watch Baby Girl during the days and most nights. When Baby Girl get to see Black Mama on the weekends, she tell her:

"Black Mama, Cousin hit me, really she do, on my face and it hurt."

Black Mama silence. She still tryin' to find her way back to herself after another breakdown. The weekend over and time to go back to Auntie X house.

It sting, Cousin X massive yellow hand upon Baby Girl face. She think it might burn forever.

"I'm sorry, I'm sorry. Don't tell my mama, okay? You okay?" Cousin X hug Baby Girl, and Baby Girl forgive her.

"Here, take this, okay? You can have it." She hand Baby Girl a dollar.

Later, Cousin X take the dollar back and laugh hard.

Baby Girl don't really know the name of this drink but know it's bitter and taste different from the sweet that pour out from Aunty X box wine that they sip on a lot. This large curvaceous bottle hold dark brown liquid. The conversation between Baby Girl and Cousin X go something like this:

"Do you drink?" Cousin X ask.

"Yea, I drink."

"Do you smoke?"

"Yea, I smoke."

"Do you fuck?"

"There these two kids caught at my school, makin' love in the bathroom."

"Oh, that's what you kids call it." Cousin X chuckle.

She pour Baby Girl a small glass of brown liquid, and Baby Girl naively chug. Bitter and dark, it all come up and out on the kitchen floor.

"I thought you said you drink?"

"I do. I'm just sick."

"Well, clean that up and then go lay down."

Baby Girl don't want to lay down. She want to play computer games. So she do, but Cousin X catch her playin' and take it as a sign of Baby Girl pretending to be sick. At dinner time, burger smells linger into Aunty X bedroom where Baby Girl play Mickey Mouse match game. She walk into the kitchen, and indeed it's her favorite: cheeseburgers and fries.

"You sick, so you cain't eat anything. Go back and play yo' games," say Cousin X.

Baby Girl stomach achin' for just one bite, but she *sick*. She not *sick*. She hungry. She go back to the bedroom and wait. She know Cousin X in the living room eating, so she sneak into the kitchen. Baby Girl check the fryin' pans, still a bit of sizzle left from the burger. She search for remnants of anything. There's one fry floating in the oil. It's a reject: small, dark and deformed. She grab it and stuff it in her mouth. Cousin X sneakily watch Baby Girl and snicker. Baby Girl don't have time to feel humiliation . . . Her face on fire again.

✦

Another day that summer, Cousin X say to Baby Girl, "Let's play doctor."

"Okay."

"I'm the doctor, and you the patient. Lay on the bed."

Sometimes it's "I'm the boy, you be the girl. Lay down."

First Cousin X lie on top and then her tongue deep in Baby Girl mouth. Then her hands start prick inside Baby Girl underwear. Baby Girl think she gon' die in Cousin X room amid her abandoned Cabbage Patch dolls and Barbies.

She got to get away. "I have to pee! I have to pee!"

"Hurry up!"

Baby Girl sit on the toilet and the pee sizzles out of her. Burn.

Cousin X get caught once. Baby Girl s'posed to be lookout, alerting her to when Auntie X come home. But Aunty X early today. Baby Girl in Aunty X room with some boy, but she see her walk past and into Cousin X room. Blankets uncovered and naked bodies exposed. The boy on top of Cousin X apologize as he stumble to put his pants back on.

"Where's the condom? Where's the fucking condom!?" Aunty X scream.

The boys run away, and the girls left with Aunty X and her anger. Cousin X dress and walk into the kitchen. Aunty X push her up against the refrigerator, she turn red, and her face on fire now too. Baby Girl feel guilty. After, Aunty X come into the living room and look at Baby Girl, she warn, "Don't you be a hoe like your cousin, you hear? Keep your legs closed."

Baby Girl don't respond. It's too late for Baby Girl. The other boy in the house in the room with Baby Girl, Cousin X tell her to *do it* to him. There others, too, that Baby Girl told to *do it* to. The times when Aunty X don't come home early.

A tightened fist to chest. Cousin X punch Baby Girl, but she don't cry or fight back. She just get scared.

Baby Girl shout, "Stop, you gon' bust my bubbles."

"What you talkin' 'bout?"

"My bubbles on the inside."

Another blow, this time to the stomach.

The bubbles Baby Girl refer to have to do with the numerous breasts implant news specials shown on television. She know her breasts ain't fully formed yet. She believe she have a bubble of silicon growing inside, and if not careful, Cousin X gon' make them explode. (She eight.)

"Go in there."

Baby Girl eyes say, *No, please don't make me.*

"Do it! Now!" Cousin X raise her hand, and Baby Girl don't want to feel that sting upon her cheek, so she go.

Later, she run out of the room because she remember how important Aunty X say a condom is.

"I don't have a condom, I cain't—"

Cousin X cut Baby Girl off, "You don't even have a period yet, he don't need one."

Baby Girl don't know what a period got to do with this situation. She go back into the room, Aunty X room. She got a large bed, it's neat and smells of incense. She walk in, and he take his clothes off. He on top of her. She look at the phone next to Aunty X bed. She want to call Black Mama. It's all blurry and dark. She want to yell. She want to say stop but only silence come.

The boy leave, and Cousin X smile. Baby Girl want to cry, but it's time to play doctor again. After, Cousin X give Baby Girl one of those baths, the kind that's s'posed to get rid of the evidence of dirty things. Cousin X put apple cider vinegar in the bathwater. After, they read the Bible. They pray together and ask God for forgiveness.

"I feel bad," Baby Girl admit.

"Me too," Cousin X say.

"I think we should tell."

"Tell? No, don't tell! We have to keep it between us, okay? God will forgive us."

"But I think God wants me to tell Black Mama."

Cousin X slap Baby Girl into another stinging silence.

BREAK

BREAKIN'

HOLD

BREAK

RELEASE

INHALE

EXHALE

BREATHE

BE&COME AGAIN

PART 2

CHAPTER 5

A Break

The previous pages were intentionally left mostly blank with words for the reader to meditate on. The space represents all that this book can and cannot hold nor carry in the be&coming. Baby Girl does not die, but she continues to struggle to find her way back to her body as girl, teenager, and then too as Black woman. I, Black Trans Man, hold it all, and this book is a bit of release for me. I will always carry the stories of Baby Girl to Black woman, not just in my memory, but in my body, in the shape of my hips, and in the way I refuse to *straighten my wrist*.[1]

I, Black Trans Man, hesitated to end Baby Girl's story where I did because, I, like Nikki Giovanni's poem "Nikki-Rosa," "really hope no white person ever has cause / to write about me . . . they'll / probably talk about my hard childhood / and never understand that / all the while I was quite happy."[2] I don't want readers to believe that all of Baby Girl's journey was trauma alone. When I think of my childhood, I think of joy and pain. The joy comes from weekly family dinners at Denny's, where Aunty G shares all the church gossip. The joy comes from playin' outside with neighbors who teach me how to drum by turning over the trash can while they practice capoeira. The joy comes from turning that same garbage can over to use it for a basketball hoop. The joy comes from family talent shows, dancin' and laughin' 'til I cry. The joy comes from church and visiting pastors who make me believe in miracles with their flamboyant preaching styles. The joy comes from getting to know the divine in the games I play outside, picking flowers and studying them. The joy comes from dreaming and not always dreaming of being somewhere else. There were plenty of times where I was simply happy to be where I was.

There were also plenty of times when I dreamed of being somewhere else and someone else, especially after that summer, after Baby Girl's body is made to hold secret-hush-hide harm. After that summer, I develop a rare disease where a huge scab began to cover my head from the center outward and my hair fell out. Doctors never figured out a diagnosis so they put me on steroids that changed my body to thick, even more like a woman than a child. I grow up chubby and then fat. I don't talk to anyone about what happened that summer except for Black Mama. Her response, I believe, stems from the traumas she too experienced and was currently experiencing just having been released from the psych ward again. I was reborn that summer, and Black Mama couldn't hold me. She was struggling to hold on to herself. Daddy was away either locked up or on another binge. I cannot remember it all. But I know that after that moment I felt *bad*. I felt like God was mad at me. I felt responsible for what happened to me in those rooms. The guilt ate at me, and I started to call home from school more and more. I didn't want to be around other kids. I spent afternoons sleeping and watching movies on VHS tapes at Grandma's house. I tried to sleep it away.

I know that my understanding of myself as a queer trans man is deeply related to those moments of trauma. Once Cousin X and I were done imagining and seeing ourselves as male hip hop stars, we played those other games that I did not like, games where I could no longer see myself. I only felt myself underneath the weight of her and her hands. The stinging still echoes. I was the girl in the scene, and I was silent, and it hurt. I held it all in, waiting for it to be over. I waited for the moment when I'd be able to see myself in the mirror again. I have great compassion for Cousin X, Black Mama, and all the women in my family. I imagine what Cousin X and I both had to think of men and boys then, always powerful, always on top, wielding a pain that women had to bear. I never want to be&come that kind of man. So instead of using this body and these hands for holding all that patriarchy asks us to hold, I decided to use these hands to create. I create poems, songs, and worlds with my words, and it is my hope that the kind of man I am always be&coming is a challenge to patriarchal mascu-linity. I am a man who is not afraid to talk about being a woman and a girl who held. As Black Trans Man, I continue to hold and carry, but I realize what I am asked to carry now is different. Different doesn't mean better or worse. I transitioned. I ask the reader to transition with me now too, from third- to second- and first-person narrative. I am ready to step into my *I* now.

I remember when Baby Girl discovered she couldn't run around with her shirt off like the boys. I also remember when I, Black Trans Man, was asked to not run around with my shirt off like the boys, and that was in a Black lesbian setting that I frequented. Two very different times and occasions, yet both led to the policing of my body. I use my hands now to create spaces where people can feel safe to take off their shirts if they so choose without fear of violence or disdain, no matter what kind of chest they have. I use these hands to pray and give gratitude for all that Black Mama and Baby Girl were asked to hold. I use these hands to dial up Daddy phone every week, an attempt to build and repair our relationship. When I use these hands to hold now, it's not heavy nor from a place of trauma, it's from a place of deep love and a desire to connect. I use these hands and my body to shape-shift myself and the world around me so that our stories of trauma be&come the exception instead of the rule.

In Part One, I share some of what needs to be lifted from my spirit, not for the purposes of pimpin' my pain but for the purposes of movin' through my shame. A release. There are so many stories I don't tell about my childhood. And there are other transitions, like the transition from public to private school. That's when I was made aware that not only was my body being made into gender female but also my language started to be policed by the educators in my life. As you transition with me from third to first person, you will also notice a change in language. How I talk and how I write changes over time as I am moved from a public elementary school in Oakland with hardly any resources to a private school that was abundantly resourced. I learned in that private school in Oakland that the way I said "I'm doin' good" was wrong. I was supposed to be *well*. They cut my Deep East Oakland tongue, mostly white teachers with good intentions of creating a good Negro. From that private school, I transitioned to an even more elite all-girls boarding school in Wellesley, MA. And from there came Williams College and USC for my PhD. My full trajectory as follows: from John Swett to Redwood Day School to Bishop O'Dowd (Oakland), Dana Hall (Wellesley, MA), Williams College (Williamstown, MA), the University of Southern California (Los Angeles, CA), and some other institutions before landing back at Williams College as assistant professor of Women's, Gender, and Sexuality Studies. I have always been in school, and school is in me. There's no doubt that these elite educational experiences changed my voice. I never unbe&uncome who I be, but I be&come more than any single English dictionary can hold.

I never knew how I sounded until I heard exactly how I didn't sound. At home, if I had a question, I *axed.* I had never been to the theater, but the *thee-ate-her* I visited often. From kindergarten until sixth grade, I attended that public school in East Oakland that was filled primarily with Black and Brown children. I was a nerd. In my public school, I *talked white*. I couldn't understand what was white about me; my parents were Black, I lived in a neighborhood with all Black and Mexican people, and my skin was just as brown as everyone else's.

I remember my excitement regarding my move to private school after sixth grade. I thought it would be a safe place, a place where all the smart kids went, a place where I'd fit in. I was sure that Redwood Day School was the place for me. Who knew that private school wasn't just for smart kids, but it was for people with lots of money! I was one of two scholarship students; me and another Black girl, Aisha, were given basketball scholarships. Aisha and I are still friends today, though we often argue over racial politics. She says that I am, *we are*, not like *other* Black people. I fight her with all that I have, but I do understand where she's coming from. Aisha, like me, often felt an outcast in groups of Black peers, and she believed private school would give her a place to belong. She never understood the compromises she would have to make. I never knew the compromises I would have to make.

The first weeks of Redwood Day School were painful; I spent most of my lunch and recess time in the girls' bathroom crying. I wanted to go back to public school. Even though I didn't fit in there, the people looked familiar, I knew what they were saying, and I understood their jokes. I didn't know how to relate to so many white people. Some might call it culture shock, but it felt like more of a language barrier.

I loved to write so I was amazed when I discovered that my academic advisor was also the English teacher. I loved J; she read my writing and was always impressed by my command of the English language on paper. However, when it was time to read passages aloud, I was constantly critiqued. It got so bad that I would cringe whenever she brought up reading aloud. Maybe she could sense my fear, because after a while, she only made me read the shortest passages. I wonder now if it was because I was uncomfortable or the fact that she didn't like the way words left my mouth. Today, my ears turn red, and my heart beats a hundred times faster than it should whenever I have to read a passage of written work aloud in a classroom.

Even though the spoken word became one of my worst fears, writing was always my passion. I wanted my words to speak for me. I remember writing the poem "Listen" during the first few weeks of seventh grade in 1997:

> *I am screaming, yet you do not hear me.*
> *When I am laughing, I am crying.*
> *When I talk you ignore,*
> *my words, my breath, my anguish,*
> *my total existence.*
> *Is it the smile on my face?*
> *The false one, the one that holds back my tears.*
> *The one that won't allow me to release my fears.*
> *Why won't you listen?*
> *These words important*

Yet, like the wind you let them fly past
without a single look . . .

It was difficult for me to communicate verbally in this private school world. I knew exactly what I wanted to say, but if I didn't phrase it a certain way, I wouldn't be heard. If *I didn't do nothin'*, it was *something*, something that needed to be fixed. I was being molded, and it just seemed too hard to rebel, so I decided to remain silent. I would let my writing speak for me. I fit into this private school world on paper, but there was very little room for my voice.

I later graduated a Redwood Day School superstar. All of my teachers were impressed by the growth I had made academically and socially. For high school, I went off to a prestigious boarding school in Wellesley, MA. This was not as hard of a transition as Redwood Day School, because by then I had learned the art of the chameleon. I could fit the mold of any situation; I could take on that East Coast upper-class vernacular quickly.

On breaks, I visited my teachers at Redwood Day School, and they were all impressed by my speech. I sounded sophisticated, like I was really going somewhere. The principal asked me how I was holding up on the East Coast, and I replied, "Well, I'm doing well." He looked at me and said, "They're doing a good job with you." I felt proud. I was fitting the mold of private school success.

At the same time, I remember hanging out with my cousins during these breaks. "Oh, you still got your white people accent on, you can drop it here." It scared me because I could drop it, and for a moment I did, but I knew that once I left, I would have to put it back on again. I wondered if there would ever come a time when I wouldn't be asked to *drop it.* I could never drop what home sounds like, the talkin', the stories. It's in me always, my language, my battered, blessed tongue.

I talk to Aisha these days, and as much as she insists upon our difference from *other* Black folk, she continues to *axe* questions.

I don't correct her;
Her axe is a weapon she doesn't even know she fires.
And
I still ain't gon' say it
The way you want to hear it
Hear it?
HERE it!
Robbed.
ROBBED tongues
LYNCHED tongues
BLOODY toNGUeS
BEATEN Tongues
Robbed, Lynched, Bloody
AND Beat-in! TONGUES
But STILL
Like dust we'sa risen'
We still BE

WE still be

Talkin'

Rappin'

Makin' it known

Dis here-you-hear is

Black word always transWorlding

Be&coming

Imma say it dis way

CUZ dats the way it flow through MY heart-hurt

Trans

It flowed B(l)ack

Through so many before me

Black people

Black Americans

AMERICA

Dey done took Africa

Put them on a ship and told them to call it home

'Til plantation time

Or they just rip out they tongues and jump,

Take their bodies into their own hands and toss

    'em overboard

Into the TRANSatlantic

A refusal to engage and a dream of radical

    elsewhere days

And I cain't let it go

Unheard

Imma write it the way I speak it

The way I heard it

Like MOTHER HARPER
In front da chuch
I know you hear WE in this written text
The same way I know you hear
BARAKA, GIOVANNI, and WALKER
The way you hear PAC and KENDRICK
Tryin' to knock some sense
Into backwards notions of BLACKNESS
Just like dis
I know you here and you heard
The word but Imma
Write it down, Right it now
Just to make sure you know
It's real and it means somethings:
Black English, Black language, AAVE, Ebonics
whatever you want to call it
Black soul revival
Black Trans survival
Black word [. . . not word . . .]
be&come Black worlds.

We, you and I, reader, are transitioning together. I have so many stories about education and language, but for this time, all you need to know is that education played a major role in the way that I relate to language and to myself. Maybe those stories will come out in other books, but that is not the story that came to be told right now. And, though it is hard to hold, all that is the story that has been presented to you thus far, it is not the only story I know and hold. In the midst of devastation, we still play, we imagine, we create, and we build.

Baby Girl transitions to girl, woman, and from there, she later transitions to he/they, Black Boi/Black Trans Man. These next chapters are written in first person. The voice shifts as I have shifted. I have stepped into the agency of my *I*, my voice standing out front, in and with this body that changes in and over time. In Part Two, I grapple with change even as I know it is a constant presence in my life. I look to my body for a home that I can hold on to when I have flashbacks of being Baby Girl. But my body betrays me as home, stable and secure. My body breaks, breaks down, just like Black Mama. My body shrinks so that I slip the grasp of any hug. My body bends and collapses before it comes together again and again.

I learn Baby Girl's dreams of home and family are never made manifest because they are built on romanticized patriarchal lies that make believe family can exist bountifully underneath carceral confinement. My body is the only home I own, and sometimes it don't do what I tell it to do. Sometimes it grows big, bigger than ever before, and I cain't stop it because that's just the way some of the *medicines go down* as doctors try to regulate my bipolar brain. I've met myself losing it, and there were no women in white to build a circle 'round me, but there were my people, my queer kin who helped to build a new shape 'round me. When I was thirty-three, I started to experience breakdowns like Black Mama, which had always been my greatest fear. But after being hospitalized, one, two, three times in three years and feeling the pull of the straps holding my body in place as I scream, as I wail, while doctors and nurses inject me with something that's supposed to calm me down, I turn up. I'm not afraid no more. And always after the mania, there comes a turn down that goes to the depths of *Dear God, please kill me.* I never knew such lows. I become a Donny Hathaway song, *Givin' Up.* Gone. Lost. Recovery. Repair in despair. I throw up my hands and ask God to take this body away. Body is not home. Body cain't hold nothin'. And body can only hold, like Black Mama's house collecting stacks upon stacks of stories. Too much. My life post–bipolar diagnosis requires deeper surrender and faith. Faith that Baby Girl had because Black Mama, Aunty G, and grandmas hand it down to her. A body made home is a lie, because home is a lie. The body is real, and my body is alive now, and that is hard to believe after all the wishing for an end that I've ideated. I'm still here. These next chapters are about be&coming in this body of mine as it continues to change because of gender transition and also the aftermath of my bipolar diagnosis.

Now that I have be&come a man, I don't always quite know how to love the little girl that I used to be. Her name was Kiana. Sometimes I don't even know how to say her name out loud anymore. Or when I do say it, I say it with a stone heart as not to awaken all she had to bear. Sometimes when I'm stressed, I get to smokin' too much and mixing genres of music like a Long Island drink, going from gospel, to trap, to the Bay, to some islands I ain't ever been to. Sometimes when I'm stressed, the music becomes too much, too many mixed messages, so I only listen to gospel and think of Grandma prayin'. Baby Girl and Black Trans Man believe in Jesus and Ancestors and other spiritual and healing modalities. Black Trans Man knows how to pray, I just do it silently now. Baby Girl and Black Trans Man stay dreamin', knowin' that it's only a matter of time before:

The pipe, the gin, the pipe, the gin
And ooooh chiild, yo' eyes ain't gon' open again
And that crackhead Ricky singin', ". . . child. child you
*   just cain't win!"*

Flashbacks. Memories. PTSD. Therapy. Be&come a healing journey, perpetual.

I practice giving Baby Girl sweet kisses and good nights, and I will continue to do so until it be&comes natural. Black Trans Man is the sweetness of Daddy and the steadfastness of Black Mama. I am the mellow in Black Mama and the laughter in Daddy. I am also their rage, turn-up, impatience, and frustration. I am also so many other things that I'm working to be&come, unbe&uncome. I ask God to give me patience and a sound mind for it feels as though this world is a crumblin', but I stand in faith. I'm livin' on a "BUT GOD!" And for me that's good. I have been broke and broken. I have put myself back together again in the breakin'. A break ain't always that bad, but sometimes it is. I have learned to remember this: We do have the capacity to heal in the break too.

CHAPTER 6

On and In Transition

W*hat are you? Boy or girl? Woman or man? I walk through the world as people shuffle pronouns upon my body casually as if they know. And then they change their minds. None of these and all are who I am. But how does one articulate this? I sat with my partner this morning, and we laughed. As a joke, I started to tell her I feel like a single . . . and there was the pause . . . person. She asked, "You didn't know whether to say man or woman, huh?" I nodded in agreement.*

It's one thing to walk through the world while others constantly mark you and (pro)claim you he or she when neither of those alone stands correct(ed). Both leave the other's body and carve out a piece of me that is only ever what they can see with dichotomous eyes. What does it mean that, when I talk about myself, I sometimes stumble upon silence as the word woman and also the word man both seem to somehow forget or disavow something so central to me, which I have not been taught to name or recognize just as most of us in this world? What does it mean to live in ambiguity yet demand recognition and respect? How can

I ask for recognition if I do not yet have the words to teach you, to give you me? This whole person.[1]

🐾

When I went in for my first appointment, the doctor asked me how long have I felt this way. When I responded by saying since I was fifteen, she remarked that that was a red flag for her. Most people will say they have felt this way their entire life—out of place and in the wrong body. I responded by saying, "Well, I really liked girly things growing up, but I felt most like a boy in drag. I liked it, but that never was all of me." I didn't say anything else, but I thought perhaps this might not be all of me either.

I grew up a Black girl and woman, and somewhere in there I chose to be&come a stud, a masculine-identified woman, masculine of center. I say "I chose to be&come a stud" because it wasn't something that just came naturally to me. When I was in my late teens and early twenties, I played with gender, wearing skirts on top of jeans and baggy shirts with a bright red fro. I hung out with the queer youth group at the Pacific Center in Berkeley when I was in California on breaks from school. It was there I was met with the most questions about my gender: "What are you? A sporty femme? A tomboy? A . . . ?" I didn't know what I was, but I thought I knew what I wanted. The first date I went on was with a tall athletic stud. She knew who she was, but she didn't know who I was, though she tried to box me into a femme position, opening doors, paying for dinner, doing all the driving. It wasn't me. It felt too confining. I felt like I had no room to play, to be all the things I carried in that particular relation. That date helped me to make the decision and the transition to be&coming stud myself. I didn't want the attention of other studs, so I had to be&come one. I learned from my peers a particular kind of Bay Area swag that was steeped in patriarchal masculinity. I remember watching a stud slap her femme girlfriend for making her *look bad* in public. I remember watching and not saying a thing. Observing toxic masculinity without men was normal then. I didn't know much, only that I wanted to be on top in this community. I worked hard to be&come stud gentleman. There were also older femme woman who taught me how to be&come stud: "Always walk on the outside when we're walking on the street" and "Always open the door for me." I let go of my attraction to other masculine people because it was more than frowned upon in my queer circle: "That's gay!" The policing of my desire was both internal and external. My stud life was colored by misogyny and patriarchal masculinity. I would eventually learn how stud was a confining role similar to femme, and I wanted to be able to move. I wanted a flexibility that my queer and straight worlds both didn't have the capacity to hold.

♣

Gender is the poetry each of us makes out of the language we are taught.

—LESLIE FEINBERG

127

*We are meant to be witnesses to a possibility which
we will not live to see, but we have to bring it out. It
has nothing to do with you and nothing to do with me.
It has to do with what we know human beings have
been and can become, and that is so subversive that
it is called poetry.*

—JAMES BALDWIN

I am a poem be&coming. At twenty-five years old, I've been
taking testosterone for four months now. I started this journey not knowing what to expect, not knowing exactly what
I wanted for sure, but I knew that this would be part of my
journey. Every Wednesday, I give myself a shot and wait to
see what changes will occur that week, if any. A voice drop?
Some facial hair? A new muscle? More horniness?

So far the changes have been slight, but more often
than not I am being perceived as male now. More often than
not I'm being perceived as a fourteen- to sixteen-year-old
male, which is not much different from before the hormone
therapy when I identified as a stud. Imagine what it feels
like when the plumber asks my partner, "How old is your
son?" Do I really look that young? Because she definitely
doesn't look that old.

As I be&come more *masculine,* I realize the pres-
sures of patriarchal masculinity and its limits in ways
that I couldn't see before. I in no way valorized patriarchal masculinity, but as a female-bodied person who was
also *masculine* presenting, I found a type of freedom in

exploring *masculinity* that I couldn't find in *femininity*. *Femininity* was what had been ascribed to me from birth. I was the little girl with the big fancy Easter dress and frilly socks. I always had a purse, a doll, and sometimes white gloves. And I loved that; I loved being girly. I can't remember when I realized that that was a performance directed by my mother yet embraced by me.

I have had many transitions in my life. I remember when I bought my first outfit that was all men's clothing. It was a simple black sweater and some khaki pants from the GAP. I was in my first year of college. I remember getting a compliment from someone and feeling better than I'd ever felt before in my own skin. It wasn't just the compliment, but it was the fact that I could look at myself and feel good. I felt comfortable, pretty, handsome, tall and strong. I was wearing clothes that fit me in so many different ways. I spent most of my first semester in college changing from femme to super stud, and in the end, the stud won out. I loved to look good in men's clothing. I wore bright colors and patterns. I was coordinated from shoes to accessories. Like my daddy, looking good was important to me.

During those years in college, I was sometimes mistaken for a boy, and it angered me. It angered me that people's understanding of male and female was so limited—I believed that what we needed was a broader understanding of woman and man; we needed more expansive definitions. Cisgender women can perform *masculinity* just as cisgender men perform *masculinity*.

And yes, cisgender women can embody and enact patriarchal masculinity too. I wanted to make sure that everyone knew I was a woman. I wanted to challenge what we think of as man or woman, in hopes of maybe disrupting both.

One of the most liberating things happened early on in my stud life—a gay guy hit on me. Here was a moment when I didn't want to announce my womanness and challenge his assumptions of what men and women could be. I just enjoyed his brown eyes locking with mine. I learned then that gender and sexuality are two different things. Even though for me they were so intertwined. My choice to be&come stud was of course partially dictated by my desire to not be romantically desired by other studs, because I had seen too many studs do harm to their partners and each other. I was not that kind of stud, but I still kept my desires for masculinity to myself because people got jumped over that kind of line-crossing in my Black queer community.

My attraction to masculinity, gay boys, studs, and other trans men has always been there. As a teenager, I'd bring some flamin' Black boy to my family events. And people would ask, "Is he gay?" I defended my boyfriends, saying "No!" probably because I had hoped they'd really be my boyfriends. But the effeminate Black boys that I brought home when I was younger were just my friends. I'd spend hours daydreaming about being closer to them even though I didn't know what that might look like. It was definitely a desire that I'd dare not explore as a *masculine* woman, stud, because it could get my stud card revoked.

130

During those first three years of college, I had long locs. I wanted to cut my locs off, but I was afraid that I might seem too *masculine*. So I transitioned again. I cut off all of my hair and got rid of all my men's clothing. I traded them in for tight dresses and heels. Some of my girlfriends even showed me how to use mascara and eyeliner, which I absolutely adored. For about nine months, I was a *real woman*. I received a lot of attention from men, but I didn't like it—I wasn't attracted to straight men. My adult transition towards *femininity* ended after those nine months, and I reflected upon it as a fun experiment. It had felt like I was playing dress-up. The whole shift from *masculine* to *feminine* started after Halloween when my friends and I decided to swap clothes. I'd be femme, and someone else would be stud for the night.

As I sit here today and think about my gender journey, I realize that it is all dress-up to a certain extent, though some things are normalized so we don't have to think about them as such. For example, a cisgender man wakes up and puts on a suit and tie—no big deal, right? Another cisgender man wakes up and puts on a skirt and heels—we turn our heads. Both people made choices, but the first choice does not cause us to think twice because that's what we have been taught is normal. Both acts, however, are performances or costuming.

As I am read more and more as male, I realize how both *masculinity* as ascribed to men and *femininity* as ascribed to women are both limiting. The other day I had an elder woman call me over to her porch, "Young man! Young man!" I went over, and she asked me to move her wheelchair from her porch to the backyard. The wheelchair was heavy—it was really heavy! But I felt like I had to do it; otherwise, I'd be failing as a man. The truth is that we all are failures of any ideal *masculine* or *feminine* being. We all have had moments that expose the failures of this dichotomy.

So then I have to ask myself the hard question: What is transitioning about? I don't think I'll feel more hopeful about gender as I become more integrated into one category (male). What am I to do about patriarchy and sexism? How am I implicated in these as I start to gain male privilege myself? How had I already been implicated in my stud life? I believe that my masculinity should not come at the cost of devaluing anyone else's femininity, masculinity, or anything else. I am a trans man, and that term to me is based upon movement and change as a constant. I'm a moving man, in search of freedom that can't be found by checking any box labeled M or F or even nonbinary, for that matter.

🐻

I have been on hormones for over ten years now; no beard, no boyfriend, and I still struggle with internalized patriarchy and heteronormativity. Though it's rare, I am still sometimes read as Black woman, and I'm still working to love her. When someone I don't know sees me and calls out

132

"woman," it says more about their own experiences with gender, what they have come to know as the possibilities for man or woman, more than it has to do with my *failure* of manhood. I had to learn that. I am a man. I am a Black Trans man, and I'm working on loving myself and those around me better.

Once, when I was riding on the train in Chicago, my best friend Jay reached out his hand towards mine to hold. And, without thinking, I snatched my hand away so quick. The stud memories lived in my body. Masculine people don't touch each other like that, at least not in public. It was okay to have some fun with other guys late at night and in dark basement rooms, but our love wasn't made for the light. That internalized homophobia is in me, and I continue to move through it by loving more fiercely, by working through the shame and the real fear that showed up in my body when Jay reached out to hold my hand. I was afraid of what other people might do to us, the possible violent response to Black men loving one another publicly. So I stopped it. Though I continue to limit my desires for masculinity as a way of protecting my own fragile manhood in this patriarchal order, it remains something that I work to unbe&uncome.

CHAPTER 7

Black Healing Matters

Black Mama wasn't a slave. She was and is a Black woman. Black Mama wasn't born in 1848 when Dr. James Marion Sims, known as the father of gynecology, was using Black women's bodies to make technological advances that would eventually be used for the sake of white women's care. Black Mama was born in the fifties. She was a Black girl, and she be&come a Black woman. Not a slave but the gynecological technologies still took hold of her body and inflicted a particular kind of pain. The doctor was afraid of what else might grow in her body that she did or did not want to keep. It was the eighties then, and white doctors knew Black women could feel pain, but they still stuck to scientific racism that led them to believe in the superwoman Black woman: "You can't feel this now, can you?" Never waiting for Black Mama's response, which came in the form of silent tears, the doctors chose not to listen, not to see, and ultimately not to feel.

Black Mama felt pain, labor and the labor of nonla bor, wanting and not wanting to hold. Choice was never certain. It could be Papa or Granny or sister or sugar Daddy who begged her to keep it, to hold her baby when she was the one who craved and needed the holding. She had the babies. The ones she had. Even though her babies sometimes got dropped or left because of all that she could not hold. It wasn't because she didn't love her babies; it was because she had lost her capacity to carry, as in *to hold* but also as in *to carry on*. She so often desired a break from the work, and the daycare, and all the things. She desired a break but not a breaking. Yet the breaking swallowed her whole. This turned break on its head. Break was not easy, was not sunshine, laughter, and beaches. It was the break, like the breaking of flesh when the bone ruptures the skin and something that's supposed to remain on the inside comes out with a bloody fierceness. She landed in a cage of her own, not like Daddy's jail cell but close.

Years later, Baby Boi, Black Trans Man, me, *I* would find myself in that same cage as Black Mama. Breaking. Broken. Bone protruding from flesh, an uncontrollable piercing. I was trapped in a body that could no longer hold onto itself. I was trapped in a ward, a psych ward, for those who could no longer hold themselves together. They fed me pills and dressed me in paper blue clothing. Underwear made of thin mesh netting. I had landed in my greatest fear, my darkest nightmare. I was Black Mama. I could no longer hold like Black Mama. I'd been pushed to the edge of skin that held me together.

When I was Baby Girl, I remember visiting Black Mama after her breakdowns, and I remember being so afraid of her, not knowing who she'd be or what she might say. I

didn't know if Black Mama would remember me after all
that had happened to bring her to that point. The pills, the
tears, the goodbyes, the swollen fingers, the fast driving.
I didn't quite know who Black Mama was anymore. I was
afraid of the room and the bed and all the blue and white.

Now I was the one in blue surrounded by white, and
Black Mama came to visit me every day. I'd tell her about
secret plots, that the doctors and nurses were trying to
kill me. She tried to soothe me, but it wasn't enough to
bring me back. I attempted to escape multiple times, and
one time I made it to the elevator, squished between the
doctors and nurses. I had no idea where I was going, but I
knew I was getting out of there, until a nurse recognized
me and my blue uniform. A nurse brought me right back
to my caged-in arena. I wasn't eating. The food there was
plastic, tasteless, slop-like. This was in the Bay Area, my
second hospitalization in three months. The first happened
in Williamstown in the mountains, but that's a story for
tomorrow or later. Now I was in a place where fights broke
out. Where people wandered around yelling and talking to
themselves. I gave all my food away to the biggest guy in
the place because that's what I had seen in prison shows—
make friends with the big guy, and no one will bother you.
And it worked too. There were old white men with their
teeth falling out, one missing an ear, and they called us
boys, all the Black men. Each demanded that a boy sit next
to them at mealtimes, and sometimes they even demanded
to be served. They were ignored, but they were present.

137

What possible healing could take place in a place like that? Trauma on trauma on trauma? Baby Boi/Black Man wasn't thinking about wellness, I could only imagine escape from this place where I didn't belong. It wasn't prison, but it was confinement. There were pastors and priests who came to pray with patients. I enjoyed that. There was art therapy during which I simply sat looking out the window as people made things. I couldn't wrap my mind around being inside. I felt guilt and shame. How could I have hit rock bottom at thirty-three? It was supposed to be my Jesus year. Perhaps it was a kind of death as I awaited resurrection.

There was a psychiatrist who visited me, but I remained silent. A white man dressed in clothes that looked like they came from my closet. I hated most the doctor's socks and shoes, because I had some just like them, but now I was draped in paper blue. Humiliated was all I could feel, and nothing this doctor said could save me. The psychiatrist called me Doctor out of respect, but it didn't matter much, it didn't give me my dignity back. It was gone. I was demoralized and baptized in the deep waters of shame. Drowning. And afraid of what might happen to me in that place. I barely slept. My room had a toilet, and there was a hole you had to place your finger in in order to flush. I was convinced that the hole was a camera, so every time I went to the bathroom, I'd stuff the hole with paper towels. I was so afraid and alone. The bathroom door stuck to the wall with magnets. I spent a lot of time removing and replacing the door, which looked like a thick yoga mat. There was nothing to do but dream of being somewhere else. I was breaking-broken, and it was not a break.

And one day Baby Girl grew up to be he/him/his even though the world or my family or my lovers didn't recognize me as such, I decided to recognize himself—gave myself a new name and a new body. And it was in this new body that I learned just how much like Black Mama I could be. I too lost it, but it wasn't safe, wasn't expected, and I had no way of holding myself and the people around me. I tried, but all of the tools weren't enough—or we just didn't know how to use them, how to speak those tools up on my behalf. I had lost his mind, or the world had gotten to me and pushed me to the edge.

There was so much Black death surrounding me in life, in the news, on Facebook and Instagram—there was no running away for me. It wasn't hard to believe that I too might be on someone's assassination list. I did hang with radicals and revolutionaries, and we mostly talked about healing, but I wasn't well, didn't know how to ask for help. I was also living in an invalidating environment: I was a beloved professor to my students at Williams, yet a nuisance to many of my colleagues who always believed I was crazy, always playing loud music, but I didn't care about that. I controlled my image and didn't mind if white folk thought me a bit crazy. It wasn't until I lost control that I or my loved ones thought, *You're out of control*, and again had not the language to say *You need more help!* My inability to see past my trauma of red, white, and blue lights calling me by the wrong name and telling me to move along caused me, too, to forget my name and, thus forgetting my body, I forgot to eat. I forgot to sleep. I started to forget others' names, I started to forget things that perhaps I'd never remember again. And I started to remember things that I thought I'd forgotten for good. I had to accept the reality of knowing not knowing. And I grew a compassion for Black Mama that I never thought was possible—not a complete forgiveness but a compassion, a softness. I still needed to distinguish myself from Black Mama because I didn't want to go on forgetting who I was: my name, my love for people, music, and the mountains, which all seemed to disappear after his moment of losing it.

It was November of 2018 when it first started, when I stopped sleeping and eating, when I started walking around campus hours before classes, holding that stolen hotel Bible in my hand. I wondered if maybe I could teach any class from the Biblical text, but I never tried it out. I remember bringing the Bible into one of my classes called Queer in the City because many of the students who took the course were homophobic, even calling me faggot after class. Their first essays had been riddled by Biblical verses that proved to students queerness or gayness was unholy, just plain not right. So I brought that class the Bible to help them understand that everything the Bible commanded wasn't always so constructive, especially for Black folk. I read that class the classic scripture about slaves obeying their masters and asked them what that meant for their lives as Black people, Brown people, women, and the students grew quiet not wanting to have to admit that the texts that they held so tightly to for their logic could betray their very own rights or freedom.

But this was a new day and I was no longer a postdoctoral fellow teaching a class with half athletes and half queer students. I was now teaching in an institution where most of my students were open, seeking theoretical challenge, there was no challenge to the rightness or wrongness of queerness when I met these students in the White Mountains of Williamstown. They were mad, and I carried the Bible along with my other essays and books, because in his moment of breakdown, I clung to the text that made me feel most safe, even if it did at times betray my very being. I started calling my Dad first and asking to read scripture on the side of the road. Colleagues stopped to ask me if I was okay, and I said I was fine, just a moment on a rock praying with my father, I said, as tears came down his face. This wasn't the first time I had been hurt by an academic institution's transphobia and anti-Blackness. It was pervasive, and I could no longer stand the cold. The cold of the Williamstown winters and the cold of some of my colleagues and the institution itself, so I did what I knew to do—what Granny taught Black Mama and she taught Baby Girl: "Take it to Jesus and write!" I wrote day and night, I couldn't stop, I couldn't stop to eat, I couldn't stop to sleep. I began to carry a cough that seemed to get worse as the days went on, and the fear of being shot by a cop or an angry colleague became greater. It escalated. I was holding students. Queer students. Trans students. Black students. I was organizing with BYP100 on the healing and safety council, ironically. I was just doing too much, and I crashed hard. My body started to wind down, and soon there would be a complete stop, a complete refusal, and an inability to move.

It was an evening that I can remember. Walking in the woods. Believing that someone in my family had been murdered by the cops, I began to cry, and walk, and pray. And, as I walked, I stripped down to nothing, leaving my clothes like breadcrumbs on the side of the road until I made it to the top of some mountain where I decided to pray some more. I walked on the ice-cold roads barefoot but could no longer feel the cold. I prayed for my students and for all the people I had lost or felt I was losing, I cried out. I cried naked in the woods until someone came to take me away. I felt it coming long before it happened, I had already known what it was like to be put out on the side of the road because I had become too much to hold for my lover. And that evening I was first arrested then hauled off by an ambulance to the hospital before being moved to the psych ward. I didn't talk to anyone the first day, I was afraid of every white person I saw. I wept. Fear rumbled throughout my body. I had never been shaken quite like this before. And three days later I was back in the classroom and teaching, but the breakdown was just beginning. Months later, I'd find myself walking up and down East 14th Street from night until morning. I ran but didn't know from what or to whom, I was just afraid and didn't know how to stop walking. I walked from the lake to Black Mama's house (eight miles) all night. Back and forth and I saw so many people, I remembered the train tracks that Daddy told me never to go to alone. But I was alone now, and my feet were starting to blister. When the sun came up, I decided to walk to the airport, again not knowing where I was going or why. I walked over a speedway, I walked in the road as cars drove past me. I got to the airport and was confused. Was I supposed to be going somewhere? I walked throughout the airport and considered entering the security check, but security reminded me of cops so I then became afraid again. So exhausted, I sat in a wheelchair next to the baggage claim, until an airport guard told him me I'd have to leave if I wasn't traveling. I left immediately and walked to Black Mama's house. Two friends would later come to take me to another hospital. I didn't understand, and I couldn't see what was going on around me. I began to think that everyone was trying to kill me. My second break in three months. The doctors deemed me bipolar, and I was in the hospital for seven days before I was released into Black Mama's care. One day before my thirty-fourth birthday. I still wasn't seeing clearly.

I wouldn't remember until six months later that Black

Mama cared for me for three weeks before I went back to Williamstown to move my things into storage. How I did it on my own, no one knows. I drove from Williamstown back to California, where I then rented a room from my cousin for the next four months. I stopped eating almost completely then, I still wasn't sleeping, and now, instead of excited, all I could feel was shame and sadness. I was alone in a room and in bed all day, I barely left the room, and I hated when the sun came up, because it just reminded me again that the days were passing, and I was doing nothing, could do nothing. I couldn't eat. I couldn't sleep. I couldn't cry. I couldn't write. There were so many times that I thought about ending it all, but I could never decide the best way to go about it, and there was still a small piece of me that was hanging on to a god Black Mama had given me. It was a god that called for me to hold on even in this, the darkest of hours. I was given every medication by a doctor who didn't listen, a doctor who simply said, let's put you on a higher dose—I became more ill. I still could only sleep two to three hours a night, and I had never experienced the kind of anxiety I started to experience then. The anxiety came with vivid dreams, dreams that everyone around me moved forward while I lay there doing nothing. This was no writing retreat, not a rest, not a break. I began to believe it a punishment, and I ruminated on what it was I could have done to put myself there, alone even when I was not. Sadness pressed down on my chest so intensely, and I had no words to describe the urge to jump out of this body and disappear. I felt shame and guilt for how I had lost it at work, how I had let down so many people I loved. I could no longer accept love, because I didn't believe I deserved it. In my own eyes I was a failure, and that is all I could see and believe, and my punishment was the morning, the dark room, and the starvation. I began to lose weight, pound after pound until my clothes began to swallow me like some deep ocean wave. I didn't know what to do with this sadness that I had never held so heavily before. And I had held sadness, I had held trauma, and now it began to spill over my body as I felt the years past and present collide. I could no longer balance them both; the past and present collapsed on and in me.

While I was at the psych ward in California, everyone I met reminded me of someone else that I thought I knew, some people were safe, and some people were not. I believed I was on a reality TV show that I didn't want to be on. I believed that former lovers and teachers were there with me. I believed I had done something wrong to be in this place. I believed I was in prison. After giving my food to the big guy, I was partially safe. "He's okay!" said the big guy if anyone tried to antagonize me.

Black Mama did come to visit me daily. Some friends called, but I wasn't much up to talking so our conversations were left at "Hi" and "Bye." Aunty G visited once or twice. My friends began to dwindle, and in the end, there were only a few people who kept calling to check in on me. I couldn't register that pain until much later. The love I once felt from the world was gone. I was stripped down, and in the end, it was Black Mama, Daddy, Aunty G, and a few friends who were there. They did what they could, but it was not enough to pull me together. They wanted me to be better, and I did too, but all I could feel was the heavy dread of loneliness. All I thought about was how I had lost it and how that made me a loser. I thought about how quickly I had faded away from the memory of those I thought were my closest friends. There were only a few that could tolerate my stuckness, every day the same. I wasn't getting better, and the pills weren't helping, and the dark room wasn't helping. I could hear the smile in the faces of the friends who still called to check in on me, and I wanted to borrow those smiles, I wanted to feel their joy. As the months went on, I started to learn how to remask again, but I still wasn't putting myself back together, I only pretended to not still be afraid. But I still called Black Mama to ask if I could sleep in her bed again. I was so afraid to be alone. I believed that my anxiety and sadness would win. I was lost, and there was no way out except through. I knew that California wasn't a healing place for me. I knew that I wanted to be able to return back to work, so I started to push myself to really take the walks that my best friend had suggested but I ignored. I pushed myself to stop smoking weed because it no longer had the self-medicating effect it once had, it only made me more afraid in and of my body. It now made me want to jump more.

I didn't know how to interact with myself anymore. I could no longer listen to music because every song reminded me of her. Every song reminded me of the things I had lost, including my mind. I didn't remember so many things, but the things I did remember were terrifyingly embarrassing, like when I showed up to a colleague's house that I did not know and refused to leave in a state of panic. Campus security picked me up, threw me in the back of a van, and dropped me back off at my house. I was not okay, and I would never be the same again. I had died, and I didn't know if I could be reborn yet again. Like a phoenix, but I was so tired of the burn. I didn't believe I could come back from this one, but I knew I'd have to push myself harder because the mask no longer worked.

I had to face the seed of myself, a small seed now, a fragile seed, a wounded seed. I only began to water it five months into my six-month leave, and I was afraid that it was too late. Would I ever be able to return to my life? No, but there was an opportunity to create a new one, a new home to be made out of body. In order to begin healing, I'd have to accept this even if I didn't fully believe it. I had been stripped down. I learned just how fragile my mind and heart could be, and I had never known such vulnerability. I had always been able to come back on my own. It hurt sometimes but never like this. I was in a state of disbelief, I no longer believed myself worthy of life or love and all of this because of a job, but it wasn't just a job, it was everything I had worked for to show my family that I was worthy, that I was something, someone worth loving, someone valuable to the world. But when I lost my love for music, my ability to write positive Facebook statuses, my love of the mountains, my love of love, I lost everything, and I knew I'd have to find myself again, recreate myself again. A transition that would take a whole new lifetime. I had to accept that bipolar was not just a made-up thing, that I had been manic and now I was depressed beyond what my body could hold.

I left California after six months to save my own life and moved to Chicago, where I got myself into an intensive outpatient program. I really wanted to be well, but all I could feel was loneliness. Chicago had been a home for me once, so I believed that it could again be my happy place, but when I arrived, I realized my whole body, my whole self, and all of my hurt arrived with me. A move would not be enough; I needed more help. And I fought for it. I spent my last six weeks before returning to work learning how to move with my feelings, how to hold sadness and pain. I sat in groups from 9 a.m. to 2 p.m. I had a whole team to help me work through this moment, and I felt more guilt for not having the wherewithal sooner to know how or where to get more help. I thought I deserved the pain and isolation. I thought I was hurting because I must have hurt someone else deeply. I knew that I had hurt many people before, because people sometimes hurt others. I thought about who might be able to forgive me, to release me, only to finally figure out that I was my own captor caught in a loop of self-hatred, doubting all self-worth. I'd have to face my shame, confront it, and name it. And that wasn't the end, I'd have to ask Black Mama, Daddy, and my queer kin to help too. They showed up for me, they did family therapy on the phone. After Black Mama and Daddy's first session was the first time I cried since my second hospitalization. I cried because I was learning that, as a family, we didn't have the language to hold broken hearts. They moved through space believing things would get better with time and prayer. I needed more. I had to learn how to release a new shame, a present shame. It was Black Trans Man's guilt.

Black Mama and Daddy came again to hold me, but there was a mediator this time, someone who could hold them all. This was the privilege of health insurance. It was the beginning of my healing, and it mattered. It was truly a life-or-death situation for me, and just choosing life wasn't enough. I had to re-create it from all that had happened not just in the past year but in all of my life. I didn't realize how much family had meant to me and how alienated I felt from my family, how unseen, and how I couldn't prove myself enough to be a man in their eyes simply because I wasn't the kind of man of their making but of my own. I didn't realize how much community would disappear. Caught up in their own lives, they kept going, and it wasn't that I wanted them to stop, but I wanted them to remember me. But the truth was that I no longer remembered himself. I was different now, but I wanted to be the same. What would this rebirth look like, and would I be able to handle it this time?

CHAPTER 8

My Stuff

I stood naked in front of my girlfriend between silence, tears, and a shame that froze me. She, a cisgender Black woman, stood across the room staring at my trans man body, and she loved all of it, all of me. But she too was on the verge of tears, and in frustration, she yelled, "What? What do you want me to call it?!" I had once again stumbled upon a familiar paralyzing silence. "What do you want me to call it?!" She started listing options and then it came out like a dagger, no pun intended: "Your dick! Is it your dick?!" In the past, I had had partners refer to my stuff as boy pussy, dick, cock, clit, dickclit, and for the most part, they all felt good when my lover was doing the naming. None of those names felt totalizing, final, or complete but, for the moment, a name made legible what often felt like, to me, an intelligible part of my body. But I didn't know how to confidently name what it was I actually had. I have spent so much intentional time thinking about names for myself, my person, while neglecting to name what was in between my legs because of shame and embarrassment.

When I was a child, my mom would just say "your stuff" or "down there." My dad, on the other hand, had as many names for my stuff as we have gender identity options now. There was kitty kat, coochie, coo coo, and all the other creative words he came up with. He was never shy, but when he talked about it, I was shy, timid, and scared. Using the term *my stuff* felt most safe and protected as it articulated a kind of ownership over my body that I longed for. Mine.

As I grew up, I wanted to be able to share my stuff. And I did (lol), but I never developed a language around what was between my legs for myself. As a little Black girl, me and my friends didn't go around comparing what our vaginas looked like, as many cis boys did with their penises. But when I started to transition with hormones, a growth spurt occurred in my clit/dick, and I needed to talk to someone about it. It was other trans men who talked to me about the growth, the feelings, and most importantly, how to clean myself now because smegma was a real thing.

As a young Black Trans man, I was interested in what was happening to my stuff, and I wanted to know if what I had grown was acceptable. My best friend, another Black Trans man, and I did end up showing each other our trans-man dicks, and while I thought that might be an affirming moment, it actually uncovered an insecurity because my dick was smaller than his. He saw the disappointment in my eyes and tried to assure me that I was fine, even better than good. I was a size queen, and I had internalized my smaller dick/clit size as emblematic of my failure of trans manhood and masculinity.

During this moment of trans-man be&coming (or, for me, another round of puberty), I spent a lot of time dreaming about what my body, my voice, my person would have been like had I been born a cisgender male. In one of our creative moments, my best friend and I decided to draw what we thought our dicks would look like had we been cisgender men. Our dicks became a central component of how we imagined our manhood. And the exercise of dreaming what might have been was not one of mourning what we didn't have but rather a creative exercise of imagining what could have been. To do this work with a friend was intimate and vulnerable; we were two men who hadn't had the opportunity to talk or vision *our stuff.* This was a moment of men loving each other and, as a result, building our capacity to love ourselves and our trans bodies.

When my girlfriend yelled "Your dick!" I felt embarrassed, not because she was being malicious in any way but because she could name my body and I couldn't. I looked down at my trans-man dick and couldn't help but think of the multiple micro penis jokes I had seen in popular films. And, usually, these jokes were racialized.

Fast forward a few years later and I'm on a date with a beautiful Black cis man. I ask to hug him from behind, and we embrace like that for a while. I feel my arms wrap around his thick body, and my hands start to wander. I can feel myself getting wet and hard, but I don't know this guy very well. I don't know how he feels about my body. My hands reach into his pants, and I begin to stroke his dick.

I feel envious that he can't also feel my erection through my pants. We go back and forth touching and kissing for a while until we are both facing each other naked. I notice a look on his face that reminds me of the look on my face when my girlfriend asked what to call it. I stared at his dick, I liked it, and before I could finish the thought, I blurted it out. He had a bashful look on his face, and his head bowed slightly towards the floor as he looked at his own stuff. "Really?" I affirmed my yes, and he confessed that he actually felt really insecure about it. Not big enough. I understood that but didn't say anything. I thought my little dick was speaking for itself even if I wasn't.

Two men—one cis and one trans—standing naked in front of each other confessing our shame, our fear, our not enoughness. Yet we found erotic pleasure and comfort in one another. This was one of the major moments when I realized how my dick/clit/boy-pussy woes were not simply a trans challenge but rather a gender challenge. Both of our bodies were beautiful. We wanted each other, but we also shared a moment of understanding that our stuff didn't comply with what was normal or should be. Neither of us were hung, which is another kind of beast of racialized stereotypes.

The vulnerability we shared was sweet, but I still had no words for my own dick. I could name his but not my own and partially because I was afraid of not having that naming respected.

In the heteronormative world, the question often asked is, "Does size matter?" And the default is "Yes, and bigger is better!" In the queer world, the question is not just about size; it's also about naming and having. What do I have? What do I call it? Where do we learn the tools to talk about our *stuff,* and how is this something that gets highlighted on trans bodies? But also how are these moments also challenges for cisgender bodies that do not ascribe to normative standards of what our *stuff* is supposed to be like?

I open this discussion of *my* stuff to get us thinking about this issue across various kinds of bodies. How and why are people made to feel shame about their genitals, and how does that affect our access to erotic resources, power, and pleasure? I don't want to continue to stumble upon silence when it comes to my stuff, and for my trans body, that means accepting that I can have multiple names for *my stuff*, and those names can change.

CHAPTER 9

This Black Body Just Won't Be Still, or Hips Lie

G rowing up, I remember being packed into the back seat of the car with my aunts and cousins as we planned on taking a drive somewhere, and there would always come a point when we'd start to feel squished in. Someone would laughingly blurt out, "You got them Carraway thighs!" Rumor had it that Paris, Texas, where my grandparents came from, was filled with big-hipped preachers. Pear-shaped people who loved the Lord. Those were my kin. Small on top and big on the bottom. My hips never bothered me much until I started to medically transition and realized my hips challenged a normative manly body. When I started to transition with hormones over ten years ago, my thighs started to slim down, but I still had booty and curves that often outed me as not man.

I remember watching the episode of *Girlfriends* where Joan dated a man with big hips, and he became the butt of every joke in that episode. Joan thought she might have gotten pregnant by this hippy man, and the concern among all the girlfriends was whether or not the baby would inherit those hips. Every time I watch that episode, I swallow the shame of my own hips and thighs.

I have struggled with dysmorphia and dysphoria since I was a child. And it wasn't just my struggle. I watched both of my parents' bodies change significantly over time. When my father got too thin, we always knew he was using again. On the other hand, my mother tried diet after diet and exercise programs to get the perfect womanly body, and she always thought herself too big. We'd be walking through the mall, and she'd look down at me and ask, "Am I as big as her?" My answer was always no because I knew being fat was bad, and my mother wasn't bad. To me, she was beautiful in all her body shifts.

When I was released from the hospital a few years back after a bipolar manic episode, I spent the next six months in bed and was manically depressed. My depression came with a great loss of appetite as I mostly ate slices of cheese. When I started to come out of my manic-depressive state, I realized my clothes no longer fit. They swallowed me. And when I looked at my naked body, all I could see was skin that drooped. I had no curves. I became obsessed with my booty atrophy. I was 145 pounds and 5'10", smaller than I had ever been in my life; not since elementary school had I ever been so small.

After a lot of hard work and shifts in eating habits and physical activity, I gained weight and, for the first time ever, felt great in my body. I hated that I had to go through such a mental crisis, but I was happy that I'd finally landed in a place where I felt I had control over my own body. I bought all new clothes since my old ones no longer fit, and I felt cute. Men's clothes fit me perfectly off the rack.

Two years later, after another manic episode and hospitalization, I found myself back in a depression where I was once again stuck in bed, only this time I couldn't stop eating. And similar to before, I wasn't paying attention to my body. I was too depressed to care.

I write this now as I am moving out of one of the most difficult phases of my bipolar disorder, this stunting depression. I've started looking at my body again, and I've felt horrified by what my body has become. My belly poking out proudly, and there's not enough sucking in I can do to hide it. My booty, my hips, my thighs are all here, and they make me remember how/if/when my gender fails.

In the last six months, I've gained sixty pounds. I have never been this big. And the shame I feel around my body is deeply rooted, such that I'm afraid to see people who've never seen me in this body. Afraid of what they'll say and how they might judge me for not being in control. It's not easy being a man, specifically a trans man with body. And it's not simply the fatphobia that I'm moving through both internally and externally, it's the gender dysmorphia too. In this new body of mine, I've gotten mispronouned in ways that I haven't since prior to medically transitioning, and I can't help but to think it has to do with the curves I now carry.

When I became so thin that I looked like I was drowning in all my clothes, I wasn't worried about my gender or being misgendered, though I did feel shame around being so small. Before I transitioned with hormones and had top surgery, I had imagined my trans man body being thick, as

I had been a thick woman, but I became a small guy and, after that manic episode, an even smaller guy.

Through all of these body shifts, my understanding of my manhood has shifted as well. I've mostly landed on "not good enough," but I write this to encourage me to love myself where I am, even if and when my body changes again.

I wanted to focus this chapter on hips because they are such a big part of how I came to understand who holds a woman's or feminine gender. "Those are baby-making hips," I remember hearing as a child. I didn't want to hold like that. I still don't want to hold in that way, yet I am a holder, and it manifests itself in my body. My hips are thick now. And I know the dissatisfaction I feel is not because I hate or feel fat people are less deserving. It's a dissatis- faction with walking in the world and being misperceived because of what I carry in these thighs. What I carry in these thighs is years of yearning to feel at home in this body. What I carry is a sense of betrayal that, no matter what medical transition treatments I have taken, they have failed. But it's even bigger than the failure of my body; I've internalized it as a failure of my masculinity. Even in the sharing of this story, I judge what others might think, that I'm so vain. But I push past my inner critic and share what I fear: that I'll never be man enough.

I'll never be man enough. But then I'm of course forced to ask, man enough for what? What kind of man do I want to be? What kind of men do I want to see in the future? Men who love themselves and their bodies, hips wide or thin as a rail and everything in between. Hips may hold for me a tenderness that the world isn't ready to love, but I must love in the meantime because I and they are here, perhaps not to stay, but for now, and in this moment, I long to give this body of mine a tenderness not often offered to men with body. For trans and cis folk, "no fats, no femmes" is a slogan that has been passed down over the years, and it hurts us all. The hips I now struggle to hold with compassion are my mother's and her mother's hips, but also perhaps, too, some pear-shaped men from Paris, Texas.

How do I fully love me without fully loving all that they be? How might the practice of loving my hips be also the practice of healing both my masculine and feminine energies? I am a man with body, and I'm working every day to love myself just a bit more fiercely. It is my hope that you take this as an opportunity to love yourself more tenderly because the gender binary has us all caught up in what we are never enough of. But we are enough, and we deserve to be seen in our dignity wherever our hips may lie. The work to undo patriarchy and toxic masculinity is both external and internal. I wish for us a world where we bask in the uniqueness and sexiness of all our bodies as they transform. But, more than that, I wish for us all to be able to lay ourselves down easily in our bodies knowing a safe home is there.

PART 3

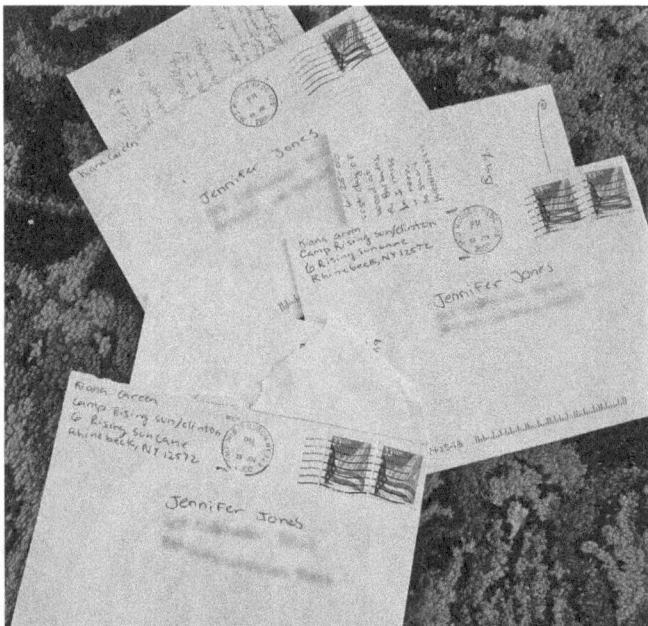

Letters sent from the author to mentor Jennifer Jones from summer camp, Camp Rising Sun, Rhinebeck, NY, 2000.

CHAPTER 10

On the Black Radical Tradition of Letter Writing

T he be&coming that is a constant in Baby Girl's story is sometimes a foreclosure, but it is also a potential opening for something else to be. In my short film "Triggers,"[1] I use bodies, movement, sound, and letter writing to examine the be&coming and intertwining of multiple Black girl stories. This film is and first came into being as a letter written to Marissa Alexander, who, at thirty-one years old, was prosecuted for aggravated assault with a lethal weapon for firing a warning shot in the air after her husband attacked and threatened to kill her on August 1, 2010, in Jacksonville, Florida. She received a mandatory minimum sentence of twenty years in prison. Alexander was released on January 27, 2015, under a plea deal that capped her sentence to the three years she had already served. The Brothers Writing to Live collective wanted to speak out on the incident as a group of Black male feminists, and my letter later evolved into a film.

Both my film and this monograph use the epistolary or letter writing to examine home, bodies, and belonging in the midst or aftermath of trauma, hence the title *Triggers*. According to Dr. Faith Harper, "A trigger is something that facilitates reliving a traumatic event. A trigger is something in the present that activates our past trauma . . . Sometimes we limit ourselves by avoiding all possible triggers, which helps in the short term but not in the long run."[2] Letter writing as a means of confronting triggers and trauma has become a major tool for me as a writer, filmmaker, facilitator, and teacher. Letter writing as a means of communication is an important component of the Black radical tradition. It is also something that I have found to be part of a Black literary tradition that tells us a lot about a writer's internal thought world and the relationships that writer has to others. The collective Brothers Writing to Live and I have all used letters to communicate to one another the stories of our lives. It is in one of our first letter exchanges in 2013 that I wrote, "But what do we do with the scars? I have scars. Visible scars from falling as a kid. Visible scars from nights of self-inflicted cutting in high school. Visible scars from my recent double mastectomy. Those scars are easier for me to deal with because I know where to find them. I know what might irritate the recent scars on my chest. But what of the scars that you can't see?"

Writing has been a source of healing for me ever since my mother bought me my first journal. Writing letters in particular has been a source of connection to others and to myself. I wanted to republish the original text of that letter here, as well as select letters and fragments I've written to family, chosen kin, and myself. Let these letters act as prayers for dynamic manifestations of Black queer futures.

Still image from the film *Triggers* by James Welch.

CHAPTER 11

Dear Marissa

Dear Marissa,

Triggers. Triggers. You pulled the trigger to save your own life. You fired shots up to the heavens, and the ground you stood upon wouldn't hold you. The court, these laws unable to recognize you and the justice you do deserve. But I will fight for you. I will write for you. I am with you.

Triggers. I know what it means. See it was just the other day, the day before Domestic Violence Awareness Month. Just outside my old house. We heard a couple yelling. She had been cheating on him. He held her phone, and I imagine he was going over the evidence. I imagine it hurt. He wanted control. She wanted her phone back, but he didn't want to give it to her. He owed her money. She wanted her stuff. He was angry. He wanted control.

Triggers. We looked outside, but there were no bodies, only voices. We couldn't tell where they were coming from, so we went back inside.

Triggers. *I can't BELIEVE you punched me in my mouth!*

Triggers. We made eye contact in the house—what do we do? We don't want to call the cops. We don't want to call the cops. We know what the cops do—

Triggers. We look outside. The screaming voices become visible Black bodies. He is short and hulking, chest out, handsome, jeans hugging. She is taller, pretty brown, eyes too hot for tears, hair short, shines fresh, a beautiful smile she possessed. And I know because I had seen her before. But now mouth blood filled, she spat and screamed back. *How you gon' do me like that?*

Triggers. Her eyes met his. She backed away. He said he was sorry. She still couldn't believe. He said he'd pay her the money he owed. She still couldn't believe. She said she was calling the cops. He begged now. He already had two strikes. She threatened and declared, phone in hand, *You going to jail today!* And he asked about their daughter. He pleaded, *Don't take me away from my daughter.* She held the phone up but never hit send. The phone was her weapon held up to the heavens, but she didn't pull.

Triggers. We were on the porch now. We witnessed. And what do you do? I asked if they were okay. My eyes met hers then. I knew they weren't. I knew it was a dumb question. He chased her around my car from sidewalk to street and across the front lawn. He caught her. He grabbed her. I yelled, *Hey! Hey!* She knew we were watching. He knew we were watching. He backed off. She came forward and, with her two fingers, struck him between the eyes. *Just leave!* I yelled.

Triggers. He backed away. Walked back to his car, and that's when I saw the other her. She was in her mother's car. She watched. She was angry. Black baby girl. I watched her watch him. She gave him a look. She cut her eyes and stuck her tongue out. Neither of them looked at her. He got into his car and almost hit the woman as he drove off. She quickly hopped in her car, pushing baby girl to the passenger seat. She sped away.

Triggers. I was triggered. I prayed for that woman. I prayed for that man. I prayed for that baby. I cried for that baby. I was that baby. Protesting the abuse of a father on a mother.

Triggers. Shock. Frozen. I went back. Watch. Witness. War. In home. Home? In war. Protest. Still, I feel weak. Small.

Triggers. Baby girl's eyes met mine, and I was reminded. One night. One night. I was nine. I was eleven. I was—Baby girl's anger. He had returned after having been gone for so long. Three weeks. Four weeks. Mom called. Maybe he had gotten locked up. She was stressed. She was mom. I was stressed. Maybe he was dead. I hoped for prison. I prayed for prison. At least then we'd know he was somewhere. Alive. We could write at least. But, in his absence, I wrote letters to the wind. Waiting for a response.

Triggers. A pounding. A knock resounding. The door. *Praise God.* Daddy's home. I didn't feel that way. I was angry. Don't let him in. Mom. *Praise God. Anyway.* But why? He came back mad. It was as if my prayer to the wind had snatched him. But he didn't want to be back . . . It was crack. Mom, don't break. Mom, don't bend.

Triggers. She let him in. He was different this time.

Unapologetic. He came in like this was his house. But this was my house. No, this was my mom's house, and I would protect her. She was silent. I wanted her to fight. She was silent. They were both in bed. He turned off the light. Mom didn't like the lights off. This was her house. He took the remote control and changed the channel. Cowboy. Action. Mom liked game shows and sitcoms. She looked blue. He looked red. Silent. I watched. This is my house. This is my mom's house.

Triggers. I went downstairs, and I grabbed a knife. Mom couldn't do it. I thought I could take this man's life. Power. I would take it by force. I stood in the doorway. Television glared through the darkness. I held the knife up so he could see. *I HATE YOU!* I declared.

Mom. Mom. I am here—don't be scared.

Triggers. He got out the bed. Took my knife. Made me feel weak. *You little b—, just like your mother!* He left. I cried. Alone. Mom lay in the dark room, still. I recovered the knife and put it under my pillow. If he returned—

Triggers.

What is justice, Marissa? I believe you should be free. I believe that the relationship we have to the state is an abusive one. We are not protected. We are not loved. We are policed. We are told fighting for our own lives is criminal.

We are forced to take it. Take it. Take it. And we do. But sometimes we talk back. We boil over. And the blood coming from our busted lips pour out onto the concrete. For some, those stains are our only tears. We fight. We are told to be quiet. We are forced to live with these contradictions.

172

What is justice, Marissa? I don't believe in trapping people in cages. I believe in freedom. I still feel guilty that the prayer I prayed for my father was prison. Trapped. I want to be free. I want to see you free.

Complicated. When that mother held that phone and threatened to call the cops but didn't. When I held that knife and imagined killing my father but didn't. When you shot bullets in the air and not in his chest. When the only option is 911, but you know they will not protect. Serve your time. Punishment. Your crime? Saving your own Black life. What justice look like? What justice look like? A poem. A wish. A hope. I share my freedom dream with you, Marissa.

A little Black girl dreams
In poems to her mother
And she answers back
I love you.
A little Black girl dreams
In prayers to her father
And he answers back
I love you, too.
A little Black girl dreams
In songs to herself
And she answers back
Sweetest thing I've ever known
Black love, my freedom
Done carried us home.
In solidarity and with love,
Your Brother Kai[1]

CHAPTER 12

Dear Mama

Dear Mom,

Do you remember the day we were driving to Hayward and I played Tupac's "Dear Mama" for you? That song spoke to all the things we've been through and gave families like ours a sense of dignity in spite of struggle and a system that worked to make us feel less than.

Mom, I appreciate you. I believe that God brought us together for a reason. We have held each other through the roughest of times. We've kept each other's secrets, sometimes to our own detriment. I know this book is hard for you to read. It is heavy. It is so heavy. But, Mom, it ain't all bad, it ain't all struggle. What I most remember of us, in our growing up together, is the laughter, the board games, the time we went to Vegas for Brother 1's twenty-first birthday and how you gave me a speech, letting me know that the child games and fun centers were getting expensive and I had enough teddy bears. You gave me a big leather jacket to wear, a hat, and some lipstick, and you handed me a bucket of coins and sat me in front of the slot machine next to you. "This way," you said, "there's a chance of you bringing something into the house." We have had so many adventures.

Thank you for always supporting me and my dreams. Thank you for all that you did for the city of Oakland as a social worker. You love hard and it's beautiful. I want you to know I am proud of you. I am proud of us. We must battle shame. We are strong, just like your alto voice when we sang in the mother-daughter Mother's Day choir at church. We still have all the memories, even though I'm not your little girl anymore. I know there were dreams you had for me that you had to grieve.

Let's grieve together. Let's build our own healing circle, Black Mama and Black Trans Man. Let us hold each other's tears and then release them. Let's hold hands and walk toward the sun or the river to weep and also give gratitude for all that we have be&come and all that is to be&come for us.

I love you, Mom.

Love,

Kai

CHAPTER 13

A Letter to My Nieces and Their Moms

Dear Nalo, Harriet, and Jasiri,

You are all so amazingly brilliant and have been since the time you were born—from the time I first laid eyes on you, from the first time we found out you were coming, from the first time I knew you were here, from the first time we met and you looked up at me with those eyes, from the first time when I held you closer because you cried, and I felt like crying but couldn't. It is not that I want you to hold me; it is that somehow your baby spirits have held me, held me here, reflected me here, and maybe you understand today or maybe you will understand when you're older, but I believe everything I say here is probably not news to you, because you all have taught it to me. I'm saying you taught me how to fall and get back up. I mean you taught me not to be shy or afraid because you were bold and always wanted to be in front, and I was happy to follow you. And I would never call you back, tell you to be smaller, quieter because of me, because of my fear. If anyone asks that of you ever— to be smaller, less of who you are or whoever you want to be—immediately walk away.

Uncle Kai is always happy to wander with you, and you all are such amazing leaders, you came here brilliant teachers, because you came here bearing your Ancestors' love for you, dreams of you, my future dreams for you, and don't be scared or stifled by what might sound like great expectations. All you ever have to do is be, breathe in, and the world exhales on your behalf, and that is an exhale of Black brilliance, I mean healing, I mean love, I mean life, I mean home, I mean family, I mean wholeness, on your behalf. Be. Have. I mean, all you have to do is be and know you have everything you need. Love. What I mean is, you came here brilliant, Black, filled with love, and that is your greatest gift. I only want and wish for you to always lean into it, the love you came here to give and to receive, it is yours, it has always been yours and will always be you, will always be us. Don't ever lose your faith in our love. You know, Uncle Kai lost his faith once, and it was you all who brought him back, reminded him of his own name, remember (twee), Ocean, swim Uncle Kai, change, transform, Uncle Kai, birthday panda, "Uncle Kai, this is just imaginary, you're okay." You helped me come back to life over and over again, and sometimes it was just my dream of you. Before you were here and after. We walked, and you looked up, and me and your mom, we stopped and stared at your shadow, and you were in awe and maybe a bit confused. You looked up at us and declared, "I am me," and we agreed. Know that I will always be here to remind you that you are you. Thank you for reminding me who I am when I forget. Know that our love will always be real, because we made it with our imaginations.

I am grateful to you, and I am grateful for your mothers. I am able to love you, because your mothers have loved me so long and so deep, they have all in their own ways, at some point or another, brought me back to life.

Denise:

We laugh, because somehow our love child made its way back to us to show us that we have always been made of love. All the things we been through . . . You were my first love, Love. Denise. Same name as my Mom. Oh, my love. How I love you for what you have taught me, for what you have shared with me. When I heard about Nalo's arrival, I can't lie and say that I didn't feel a bit sad, because I thought that it was always going to be me and you and her/him/them. And, somehow, even after our separation for all those years, no space or time could stop our love from blooming, the universe said yes . . . AND . . . the story doesn't always go the way we planned, but the universe made something more beautiful for us: a family of our own creation. Nalo is our love child. She looks like you and your people, to me, that's what I see. Your eyes. Your smile. Your cry. Your tenderness. Your sensitivity. Your strength. Your athleticism. Your longing. Your tense shoulders. Your great arm. Your speed. You. You. You. Your greatness. Your beauty. Your voice. My Love. And it is great, good. It has always been, and I hope you see how our Nalo reflects that love.

I see you now, seeing yourself in her, in her smile, in her desire to help and love others. The way she loves, she gets it from you. But she dances like her Uncle Kai (Apple Pie) ;-) Thank you for allowing me to be in your lives. Thank you for letting me love you. Thank you for giving me what I've always wanted and dreamed of. Those dreams we shared together in our dorm rooms in that purple valley. I wrote you songs, and you played rugby and sang and ran. I will always write songs for you, songs for us. You taught me how to love better. And yes, we hurt each other, but we, you, we stayed here to help heal each other too. That's our love story, and it is so grand. How God gifted us with a love child, so sweet, so wild and free, unafraid to jump in my arms, unafraid to enter the waters with me, she was never afraid, but we, you and I, were. You push me to save her and know I would never let her drown, but I see you will always catch her. Know, too, that I will always be here to hold with you our love. Remember our love is so sensitive, and it is beautiful, and it is okay for her to cry, you breathe, and I will hold her hand and comfort her, and in a minute, we will all get home, and you will rest, and me and Nalo will play. She will teach me how to talk to robots and lead us both to a future where we are blessed enough to dance to a beat of our baby's making in these bodies of ours. Thank you for making home, love, with me.

Thank you, babies, big kids, teenagers, grown-ups, loves always loved, love. Wherever you are now, if you are reading this or somebody is reading it to you, know that I love you, now and always, and in all ways. Uncle Kai will always be here to dance with you, to hold your hand when you are crying, to play with you, to dance in space and be saved from falling out of imaginary spaceships by you. Giraffes can dance, and so can we, thank you for teaching me how to move without fear. I love y'all.

—Uncle Kai

CHAPTER 14

A Letter to They Younger Self

Dear little one,

I used to know you as my little girl self, Baby Girl, and I've written to you over the years yearning to mother the wounds in you that Black Mama couldn't. You were always silly. You always held a heavy sadness too, even before that summer when hands violated your precious body. I remember you sitting on a pile of Black Mama's clothes in her dark closet and singing to yourself, "Nobody loves me, nobody likes me." You'd do that for hours. You were lonely, sad, and you missed Daddy because he had been locked up for some years. I want you to know that I love you, little one, Baby Girl and Baby Boi. But I focus this letter to you, Baby Boi. I will never leave nor forget who you are in me again. My curious friend who loves to sing and make things up. You were never just Baby Girl. You were always Baby Boi, too, or perhaps another kind of gendered baby that sought to be loved and seen. I don't know what pronouns you wish to use, so I choose they to honor all that you may have wanted to be called.

You got in trouble for taking your shirt off at school and walking around in your T-shirt like the boys. You were always there, but I didn't know. It wasn't until this last year after my month-long hospitalization for yet another manic episode that I got the opportunity to connect with you. I was at a retreat, and we were asked to visit our younger selves and have a conversation. I was shocked at what I saw when I came to visit you. You weren't Baby Girl anymore, you were little Kai, and you were in trouble, trapped in a hole, covered in filth, and your hair was matted down with leaves, twigs, and mud. You were cowered over, head between your knees, eyes closed, you had been abandoned. I left you. It was as if you were back in that closet singing that sad song. I didn't know what to call you but visualized what helping you heal might look like. You were so thin once I visioned cleaning you up, and you were scared. You didn't know me or trust me. I didn't know you were here in me, but I was the one who left you. I offered you food, but you wouldn't eat. I offered you a bed with warm blankets, and you hid beneath them. I sat there with you for a while and then returned to my adult self, my adult world. But I visit you regularly now, still trying to get to know who you are as you heal. As I heal.

This letter to my younger self is not like any other letter that I've written because my adult self is also still trying to get to know who I am as I heal, change, and come into deeper consciousness around what this thing called bipolar disorder is. It's real. The manic depression is real and something I think we've experienced most of our life. I can't say that hiding in that closet or being trapped in that dark hole-space is something I can save us from. But I can say for sure that I won't forget you again and that holding you is essential to holding my adult self now. I can help to hold you even though I know you've been so used to holding yourself.

I write this letter to apologize and to make amends, because I need you to survive. I know that you have dreams and visions that you've given up on. I know there was never much space made for you growing up outside of trauma. You had a dream of being the darker-skinned Kris from Kriss Kross. I never forget looking in that mirror in Aunty's bathroom and finally feeling lovable and likable. I want you to know that you are more than a trauma response, you are a survivor surviving, but that's not where our journey will end. You can imagine, and I will set my pen down to do this freedom-dreaming work with you.

We have work to do, and we have rests that we must take for the sake of our very own life. We've been broken down, and in building this relationship with you now, Baby Boi—our genderfull one—I think we might find our way towards our new, more tender world.

It's OK not to know what our freedom dreams are right now. I thought I knew. I put us on a track to get out of Oakland, become a writer and a professor. We did that! We did that work, but that's not where our story ends. We manifested these dreams that also doubled as ivory tower nightmares too. What I want you to know is that I will not stop fighting for us, because we deserve all the great good in this world.

I found you in that hole trapped in a nightmare of hopelessness that is all too familiar. I don't have all the answers, but I vow to you and to Baby Girl that I will seek out our love for self because we deserve it. It has never been an easy journey, but you refuse to die, and your resilience is also my resilience. Thank you.

I wish I could tell you that we've been through the worst of it, but I don't know what happens next. I can promise to center my spiritual, physical, and mental health. I can promise to keep visiting you and asking you questions about what you desire and what still hurts. I can promise to love you, and when I'm feeling hard on myself, I can promise to seek out the empathy and compassion we deserve.

I ask for your forgiveness for neglecting you, my inner child, Baby Boi who also needed care alongside Baby Girl. You were invisible to me, like I've often felt invisible to the world. No one taught me your name, but you exceed naming. You are felt. You are real. And I believe in your ability to get back up again. I will pull you up, but know that it isn't just me. There is a whole community of kin and ancestors who dream of us manifesting our wildest dreams. I will sing you sweet songs of home and heart. I will hold you.

Baby Boi, you are precious, and I thank you for taking this journey with me.

Love,
Marshall

Black Trans Man makes a slam dunk on the playground of his former public elementary school, John Swett (now Roses in Concrete Charter), in Oakland, CA, 2018. Photo by Texas Isaiah.

When, Where & How They Exit

It took them seven years to get their PhD. They finished at twenty-nine just in time to meet their goal of getting a doctorate before thirty. The journey was a tumultuous one, a break-breaking one. It was a journey that caused them to develop a nervous stutter. They didn't know what they were talkin' 'bout in all those schools that would be&come home to them.

Home be&come Redwood Day School—the private day school Baby Girl attended for seventh and eighth grades, Dana Hall—the all-girls boarding school she attended from tenth to twelfth grade, Williams College—the undergraduate college she attended and later taught at as Black Trans Man, and the University of Southern California—they graduate program. Home had already be&come all of the elite educational institutions they attended post–John Swett, the public school Baby Girl attended in Oakland from kindergarten to sixth grade. All of these elite spaces made them more self-conscious of their Black girl speak, which was not body but informed body's movement, discipline, and constriction. These institutions attempted to suffocate her

Black American East Oakland tongue in chains like "'doing well' and not 'doin' good.'"

These schools thought she was *special.* Their access to this elite education was a privilege. This access was an opportunity but also a separation from home, family, Aunty G, Black Mama, brothers, cousins, and Deep East Oakland. This access was books, bands, sports teams, student clubs, theater, mental health days, and the list could go on. This access was also trauma inducing, different from the trauma Baby Girl experienced in childhood at home. They are still recovering.

Why were they saying it *that* way? Why so many words for something so simple as *wrong* which they refused to accept as their name?[1] Their mouth overflowed with big words, terms, theories, ideologies, histories, narratives, and counter-narratives. They had traveled a long way from their journals and letters to Daddy in prison. They couldn't always swallow what was being fed to them in these academic institutions, so they choked on words. They worked to master these words, this standard English language that was supposed to set them free yet be&come a suffocating capture device. But there were always the stories and the writing, the writing and storytelling held their attention. So many stories—that's what they loved about schooling and what they loved most about family. It was the way that they learned best. Stories be&come home when body could no longer hold. Stories were Black Mama, aunties, and cousins crackin' up, drinkin' fountains of coffee, and rememberin' all together what was good or out-of-this-world-wild and then reenactin' it. Just *a-hoopin-n'a-hollerin'*! They family made up words and sometimes people on the outside may have called them *country*, but Baby Girl was always happiest in their family stories. It was the same place they felt most at home in academic institutions, in the stories of how it all came to be and the multiple counternarratives that came along with these stories, theories, and ideas.

Black Mama and Baby Girl at her preschool graduation from
24 Hour Children's Day Care Center, Oakland, CA, 1988.

Black Mama, Aunty G, and Black Trans Man at his
hooding ceremony, USC, Los Angeles, 2015.

Though writing and poems come to them in dreams, flowing easy, reading is painful for them. Ever since they were Baby Girl, Black Mama try to teach her to read *Brown Bear, Brown Bear, What Do You See?*, reading be&come a lonely struggle that she mostly kept to herself for fear of being deemed stupid. Black Mama and Baby Girl sit on the stairs next to the gas heater blaring heat as Black Mama try to guide her through all the animals *Brown Bear* see. The words feel like unsolvable puzzles to Baby Girl, and she hate being wrong. She start to boil over in her stomach and behind her eyes, the anger and frustration of not *getting it* turned into rage. This rage of feeling insufficient fill her five-year-old brown belly as she sit next to Black Mama atop the stairs, picking at the gray-stained pink carpet in between the dingy long metallic green wall heater and the two doors of the upstairs rooms. Baby Girl with all that rage in her belly, tightening, snatch the book from Black Mama's soft caramel hand and throw it with all the strength of her lanky arm while screaming, "I WILL NEVER LEARN HOW TO READ!" Baby Girl wait for Black Mama to respond, but she simply stand up and walk away. Black Mama walk downstairs to the bathroom and light one of her menthol cigarettes and try to exhale. Baby Girl sit in that cramped hallway feeling the heat from the wall heater as the smoke from the bathroom creep up the stairs. Smoke surround her body like the hug she want. Heat seep from her body. She don't know what to do with it, so she just sit there holding her breath until she cain't hold it any longer. She eventually gon' have to inhale Black Mama's smoke.

Later, Black Mama and Baby Girl convene on the bed in front of the television. They both love watching *the stories*. *All My Children* is Black Mama favorite. In the living room of aunties' houses were Baby Girl's favorite storytimes. Still, reading never get easier for them even after they take that speed-reading course, even after Baby Girl get an academic poor-Black-kid-with-potential basketball scholarship to Redwood Day School (RDS). At RDS, she get books that she can take home and write in. In fact, writing, highlighting, and taking notes in the margins somethin' that Baby Girl learn essential for *textual analysis.* She throw it in the toilet: *textual analysis.* Baby Girl always been a slow reader, and when Nice White Woman English Teacher at RDS announce she collectin' everyone's copy of *Ender's Game* and checking margin notes and highlighting, Baby Girl feel scared and sick because she don't know what notes to take, and she still have half the book left to read. But Baby Girl want so bad to be good. So Baby Girl take her book to the toilet the night before Nice White Woman English Teacher was to check for notes and let it go. After Black Mama finish her evening drag, Baby Girl go to the bathroom and hold her book high above the pink porcelain brown-stained toilet bowl and let it get wet enough. She let it soak in the toilet before pulling it out and teaching herself to believe that this was really an accident that she had no control over. She bring the book to school the next day wrapped in an old plastic shopping bag. She promise Nice White Woman English Teacher that she had indeed done the reading, highlighting, and margin annotations, but her book had fallen into the toilet ... *accidentally*. She pull the wet book out of the plastic bag and hold it out for Nice White Woman English Teacher to take a look, she look disgusted and say, "That's okay. I believe you." That's when Baby Girl first start lying to cover up what she don't know, out of fear that everyone discover she not in fact be smart like everyone had told her at her last school, John Swett. At John Swett, she *talked white*, but at RDS, everything that came out of her mouth was Black Mama, Daddy, Grandma, and Pastor. John Swett was a public school that didn't always have enough books for everyone to have their own, so they didn't get to take their books home.

At John Swett, Baby Girl real good at math. But John Swett is an ain't-shit school. Teachers do their best with what they got, but they ain't never got much. Baby Girl proud when teacher ask her to be on the Math Olympics team. She take pride in being smart. A group of students head to one of the other elementary schools in Oakland in the hills for the competition. Baby Girl ready. Excited. Baby Girl competitive. When they hand out the first round of questions, Baby Girl see symbols and a mathematical language she had never encountered before. No one on Baby Girl Math Olympics team make it past round one. Baby Girl realize then that somethin' wrong. They work so hard training after school with teacher and teammates, but when they go to the competition, what they know don't even qualify them to make it through one round. Baby Girl don't feel shame; she feel anger. She realize then that everything that they have to give her at John Swett won't ever be good enough. She was good enough. Her classmates were good enough. But what this school offered them was shameful, it was not good enough. Many of the kids in these kinds of schools get confused in believing that we aren't good enough, internalizing that as the truth of who we are. Baby Girl and Black Trans Man refuse to believe that lie.

Baby Girl in Math Olympics, Oakland, CA, 1990s.

And still reading never got easier for them, even after Dana Hall's New England all-girls boarding school elitism, after Williams College, *the number one college in the United States*,[2] after USC, after PhD and Northwestern postdoctoral fellowship. And after all that *education* they had acquired all the markers of someone brilliant, but they felt—more than anything—*stupid*, always holding onto "I can't keep up. I don't wanna get kicked out. I can't let them see me struggle. Lie your way to a win. A win is a win. A fight is a fight. This shit was never fair anyway . . ." Baby Girl cain't keep up with the wealthy, mostly white students at RDS. But, somehow, they manage to make it through school because they listen; they study personalities and spirits more than books. They always listen to the stories, whether English or math or . . . They learn how to translate everything into a story. And for them, in every story, there a lesson and a pattern. People, too, be stories, patterns, and Baby Girl get real good at reading them. She learn that from Mama and aunties and Daddy and Grandma and her own body also an essential part of the teachin'.

Stories, Baby Girl learn, not only rule her childhood world of Black Mama and aunties' gossip about the choir, so-and-so's son, and secrets that supposed to be kept but never are, especially between Black Mama and Aunty G. And everybody know, once Black Mama know, *everybody* gon' know. Baby Girl love to listen to Aunty G's stories especially, because Aunty G's stories live-action before live-action. Aunty G the eldest sister of her eight siblings, and she Baby Girl hero, because not only do she direct a daycare center for low-income children in Oakland, run two shelters for survivors of domestic violence, and direct a college scholarship for young people from Oakland, she also a performer, a singer, a dancer, a creative, a church lady, a choir member, a Sunday school teacher, a safe house for young people in the community who need family. She also have four children of her own and often care for her siblings' children as well. Aunty G an organizer even though she probably never use that word to describe herself. Baby Girl want to be like Aunty G because Aunty G also chase robbers or people who act out in front of the daycare center. Aunty G got no fear, only fight, and always a bottle of *Holy* anointed oil in her purse. Baby Girl want some of that fight, and one day they grow into it. Black Mama and Aunty G always say their daughters switched because Baby Girl always more like Aunty G and Cousin C always more like Black Mama, a homebody.

Aunty G's daycare center or The Center, which everyone call it, is right on East 14th, now known as International Boulevard, a failed rebranding attempt.[3] The Center smack dab on the corner of the stroll.[4] Aunty G an educator, and she love children, watchin' them learn and grow. It don't matter how little the resources are. It don't matter that the City of Oakland don't put a crosswalk on that corner until 2019 . . . The Center open in 1973. Aunty G make it work. It don't matter, the moments when all of the children and teachers stand on tables and chairs because they afraid of the mice scurrying about their preschool. Baby Girl and most of her cousins on Black Mama side go to The Center. Education important on Black Mama side of the family. Granny go back to college to study education at UC Berkeley after having her eight children. She travel abroad to Ghana. It ain't uncommon for people to go to college on Black Mama side of the family. Granny even got her master's degree. And so many of her offspring follow in her footsteps. But Black Trans Man the first doctor, the first PhD. And on his Daddy side, the first generation to get a degree beyond high school.

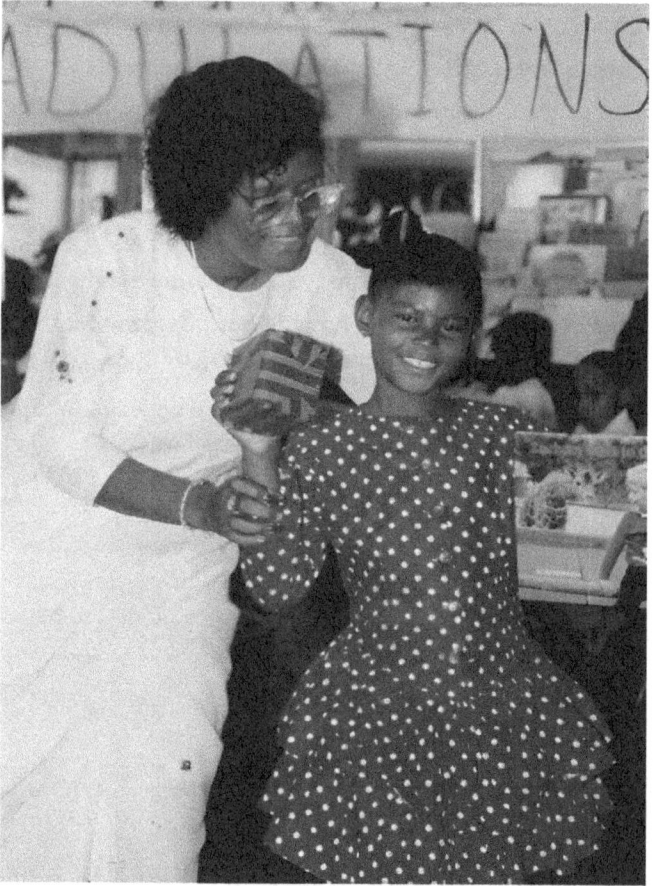

Aunty G and Baby Girl hosting the holiday event at
The Center, Oakland, CA, 1994.

Aunty G and Black Trans Man stand outside The Center, 2020.

They spend seven years—most of their twenties—in South Central Los Angeles at the University of Southern California, working towards a doctorate in American Studies. And when they defend their dissertation, Black Mama, Auntie G, and Brother 2 there. And so is all the people they had interviewed about being *Black and Gay in LA*.[5] And so is all they chosen family and friends. They girlfriend at the time Skype in and even have flowers delivered to the classroom. And of course their committee is there. They are all Black tenured scholars and one cool white feminist as a required outside committee member. The room is full, Black, and queer. "But what the hell is American Studies?" is the question many have for Black Boi (Baby Girl major in American Studies in undergrad as well). But stories—everyone understand stories, people tell and know stories, sometimes in their bodies. "A Deep Hanging Out"[6] is not surprisingly their research method of choice. It's called ethnography. One of their favorite undergraduate Black feminist professors suggest ethnography might be the academic method for them, and they listen. In graduate school, they collect stories of Black LGBT folk who mostly came of age in South Central Los Angeles in the '80s and '90s because all the books they read about queer Los Angeles tend to geographically center themselves north of Highway 10, where most of the Black folks aren't. For Black bodies, geography always matters.

Home as geography, as body, is a story to be made and remade, a perpetual be&unbecoming. It's always been about the stories for them, the be&comin'. Baby Girl learn early on how to fall in love with a tale. She learn early on how to tell a tale. She ask Black Mama and aunties to tell the same stories over and over again because she love the remembering. She love listening to them remember and how the remembering always the same and different every time. She love the disagreements over how it *really* happened and the laughter that came along with all of that. It's never really about what *actually* happened, like the fact that they really did beat Cousin Big E in Scrabble, but because he never acknowledge that reality, it's as if the story only exist in their imagination. What happen when you the only one who remember what happen?

It is always about the stories that circulate. It never matters what *actually* happened. It is the story that will be told about the event that remains imprinted upon the collective memory. And they take their love of listening to stories everywhere they go after they leave Deep East Oakland.[7] They learn through their academic study of American Studies that histories too are narratives, tales, stories, and a lot of times, they are flat-out lies! They learn from *the Abolitionists*[8] (which they'd one day grow to call themself) that theories must be guides for action, or they're bullshit![9] They sit in these classrooms, always so far away from home, family, and the words that roll off they tongue easy. The first real theorists they encounter are Black Mama, Grandma, Daddy, uncles and aunties sittin' around the table telling tales, only no one would ever read about their heroics. How Black Mama do it, live the theory that give them and their brothers life.

They be&come ethnographer because they like talking to people, regular people, everyday people and because everyday people always the most spectacular people. They learn that from walkin' with Daddy. Daddy everyday people and his family—biological and chosen—everyday people too. They don't go to college. They all everyday people, but Black Mama side believe they more *refined* than Daddy side, and Daddy feel the same way too *sometimes*. Mama never walk, she only drive.

Later on, when Baby Girl get propelled into some of the most *elite* academic institutions in the United States, there they learn and eventually unlearn *wrong* be&come their *name*,[10] or at least that's the way *good, nice, white* private school teachers said it sound to them. It is also while there that they learn a new spelling of their name,[11] Black Trans[12] love. They be&come conscious that they not just a Black poem,[13] but a Black poem in a linguistically white America that never stop cutting away at their tongue, which be a major part of their body. That's why in this book you read all the languages, the tongues that they learn and unlearn, make and remake, sometimes violently. Their tongue be&come bridge. Their tongue be&come proper and untameable. Their tongue be&come, "This what I look like when you write me down or out of history . . . Sometimes I be silent-empty-blank-white-Black-No-name-pages."

This Baby Girl's Biomythography and Black Trans

Man's attempt to grapple with all that he has be&unbe-
come. This is Black Boi's Biomythography. This is their
Biomythography and they choose this form because they
tired of swallowing all the toxicity they forced to stomach
with a "Thank you, *Nice White Teacher*." They learned about
Biomythography because legendary Black Feminist Audre
Lorde use it to describe the telling of her life story in *Zami:*
A New Spelling of My Name. This Lordian literary genre

> used . . . to explain and analyze the narratives of
> women of color and postcolonial storytelling prac-
> tices. Biomythography melds nonfiction and myth,
> while placing a personal narrative amidst the many
> communities that person exists within. It challenges
> the lines between fiction and non-fiction while also
> questioning the singularity of an autobiography.[14]

Today, Black Trans Man uses this genre—borderless
between fiction and nonfiction, not singular like autobiog-
raphy—to help him tell their story of change and life-living,
changes in and over time. There are many gaps just like the
memory lapses he experienced after every manic episode.
Many expect him to focus on his transition from "female"
to "male," but *A Body Made Home* does not focus on simply
gender-identity transition beginning with Black Boi's offi-
cial announcement, "I'm Trans!"

In theory tongue: Genders are always already in transition, and the gender binary, a powerful master, inflexible,
has different consequences for different bodies as they

change in and over time. All people are gendered subjects in the United States, meaning they are all read through the binaristic lens of male and female, masculine and feminine (and perhaps today a trinary of male, female, and nonbinary is starting to be normalized), as if these are the only possibilities for be&coming human. As if this binary does not present unstable categories that change over, in, and out of time, illuminating "a radical Elsewhere,"[15] "an unmappable elsewhere,"[17] an "elsewhere and elsewhen"[17] a "queer elsewhere of black diaspora,"[18] a "Beautiful Black Feminist elsewhere,"[19] a "radical Elsewhere . . . 'outside of homogenous space and time' [that] 'does not belong to the order of the visible,'"[20] Baby Girl, transition to Baby Girl, this not somethin' she enter the world knowin' she expected to be&come. It's something she have to be taught.

She is named. And mostly, she learn that gender, that name, Baby Girl, through the policing of her Black girl body. In theory tongue: Transition and change are all around and in us, but the visibility of transgender people in media and popular culture in the twenty-first century has meant that many have come to myopically understand the depths of transgender as white depths, which is different from Black Trans Man's theory of trans.*[21]

A Body Made Home seeks to uncover some of the different ways that bodies are made, which includes not just how bodies see themselves but also how others view them. Bodies be an interdependent co-construction. The way that one is read in the world has material, consequential effects that can be positive and/or negative and/or . . . Even when they identified as Black Woman, they dress like Black Boi, stud, which means the police in Los Angeles pull them over (. . . for no reason . . .) because they read as both Black and male, a potential threat to justice and presumable peace. In that moment, her chosen identity of Black lesbian woman and stud don't matter because, to the white police gaze, they signified Black Man, presumably cisgender and straight, which mean all their movement be furtive and narrowing they possibility of be&coming.

As a Black Queer Feminist, an aspirational politic for them,[22] they believe that stories are powerful tools that can topple hierarchies, at least ideological and pedagogical ones. He chose the genre of Biomythography because it is an offering of a unique genre of writing given by a Black Feminist ancestor that many have dared not take up. In his Biomythography, *A Body Made Home,* he asks, What are the myths about gender, race, and class that create the my&me and the we&us of Black bodies, emotionally, physically, psychically, spiritually, individually, and collectively? This text uses their stories as a kind of evidence of what had happened.[23] The evidence is not to prove what had happened as objective truth, rather this Biomythography asks its readers to release—for a moment—control, the expectation of memoir, to bring one closer, to help one to know the *real real.* Sometimes people know and " . . . see better in the dark . . ."[24]

It is true that there are things that Black Trans Man simply can't recall. Sometimes the way he recall is different from the way his cousins do. Or different from how they conceive of their story a decade ago, when they first started writing this book. They feel/felt differently about the whole thing then. Change is constantly happening over time, and time under capitalism don't stop. Time changes perspective, and it changes bodies. Black Trans Man say upon their exit of *A Body Made Home*, in goodbye tongue, in letter to reader: Thank you for bearing witness to these pieces of my story. Now, please, take my hand, gently. Let's fly away from here, for we still have a lot left to be&come and even more to unbe&uncome.

Self-portrait of Black Trans Man stretching at
Prospect Park, Brooklyn, NY, 2018.

About the Book Cover

The cover of this book was created by the brilliant multimedia artist and puppet maker from Evanston, IL, James N. Welch.[1] Welch's interest in Afrofuturism as a practice compels him to center the question "What if?" While digital pieces depict an imagined journey and arrival to a Black utopian future, his 3D art—sculptures and garments—encompass what we could have when we get there. Rather than replicating portrayals of Blackness that dwell in and glorify Black suffering, the storytelling that emerges through Welch's work uplifts legacies of joy, resilience, and creativity. His use of nonconventional materials such as coffee and recyclables underscores a Black radical tradition of creating more with less despite limitations of space, supplies, time, and freedom. There is an urgency in his work.

In the cover image, Welch wears a costume, a suit made of teddy bears that have been individually sewn on. This project explores the comforts we imagine of childhood. The bears were made to signify the playfulness of a little Black girl, but when he put on the suit, he realized it was heavy—it was sixty pounds. It wasn't easy to wear, and it wasn't easy to carry—in similar ways to Black girlhood—at times. So this suit has multiple and sometimes contradictory meanings. What is worn on Welch's head is a "scream helmet," which he designed to be a usable object that allows one to scream and go off without the sound escaping and causing a sonic disruption in public. It is usually not safe for Black people to lose it publicly because of the ramifications of what it means to be Black and angry or, even more, Black and out of control, crazy. The helmet is made to hold the wailing while protecting the wailer from judgment or policing. But this "scream helmet" also be&come in the making its own thing, unbound by even the creator's purpose. The "scream helmet" be&come an echo chamber, screaming back at its wearer exactly the thing they were trying to get out. This is another example of how the intended goal was not quite attained, but there is a lesson in "scream helmet"'s echo chamber as it can also be seen as a kind of inescapable encounter with one's sonic scars and triggers. What was meant for an externalization of wailing may provide an opportunity for an internal excavation of what still hurts. This book is an excavation of what still hurts and how one might transform that hurt into something else like healing, joy, Afrofutures, or even ...

Notes

Prelude: In the Beginning: Fast

1. Versions of this chapter were published in *Love WITH Accountability: Digging up the Roots of Child Sexual Abuse*, ed. Aishah Shahidah Simmons (AK Press, 2019) and The Feminist Wire, accessed February 22, 2021, https://thefeministwire.com/2016/10/fast-black-girls/.

2. In her senior year of college, she transitioned from stud to femme. It began as a Halloween event, where all of her friends wore "opposite gender" clothing.

3. Kai Green, "Troubling the Waters: Mobilizing a Trans* Analytic," in *No Tea, No Shade: New Writings in Black Queer Studies*, ed. E. Patrick Johnson (Duke University Press, 2016). Trans* is defined "as a decolonial demand; a question of how, when, and where one sees and knows; a reading practice that might help readers gain a reorientation to orientation. It is an analytic that has ontological, ideological, and epistemological ramifications. It is not perpetual alterity but perpetual presence. It makes different scales of movement or change legible."

4. The terms they/them/theirs refer to both Baby Girl/Black Woman and Black Boi/Black Trans Man. They is also imbued by the complicated nature of living in the United States as Black Girl/Black Woman and Black Boi/Black Trans Man and all the spaces in between. He and they are the pronouns that Black Trans Man, the author, chooses to use at the time of writing this. See also Colin Dwyer, "Merriam-Webster Singles Out Nonbinary 'They' For Word Of The Year Honors," NPR, December 10, 2019, https://www.npr.org/2019/12/10/786732456/merriam-webster-singles-out-nonbinary-they-for-word-of-the-year-honors.

Chapter 1: Home

1. Here, I reference Hortense J. Spillers, "Mama's Baby, Papa's Maybe: An American Grammar Book," *Diacritics* 17, no. 2 (Summer 1987): 65–81, https://doi.org/10.2307/464747.
2. For a short history of family visits, see "The Dark Origins of Conjugal Visits," Wilson Inmate Package Program, July 10, 2024, https://wilsoninmatepackageprogram.com/blog/the-dark-origins-of-conjugal-visits/.

Chapter 2: Losing It

1. Bruce La Marr Jurelle, *How to Go Mad without Losing Your Mind: Madness and Black Radical Creativity* (Duke University Press, 2021), 305.
2. James Baldwin and Margaret Mead, *A Rap on Race* (Delta, 1972), xiv.
3. Here, I reference Evelynn Hammonds, "Black (W)holes and the Geometry of Black Female Sexuality," *Differences: A Journal of Feminist Cultural Studies* 6, nos. 2–3 (Summer–Fall 1994): 126, https://read.dukeupress.edu/differences/article-abstract/6/2-3/126/301160/Black-W-holes-and-the-Geometry-of-Black-Female.

Chapter 3: Special

1. "Special," Encyclopedia.com, June 16, 2025, https://www.encyclopedia.com/humanities/dictionaries-thesauruses-pictures-and-press-releases/special-2.

Chapter 4: Hands

1. Here, I reference Ray Charles, vocalist, "Night Time Is the Right Time," by Nappy Brown, recorded October 28, 1958, and released as a single in December 1958.

Chapter 5: A Break

1. See also Kai M. Green, "Navigating Masculinity as a Black Transman: 'I will never straighten out my wrist,'" Everyday Feminism, April 5, 2013, https://everydayfeminism.com/2013/04/i-will-never-straighten-out-my-wrist/.
2. Nikki Giovanni, "Nikki-Rosa," Poetry Foundation, accessed August 1, 2025, https://www.poetryfoundation.org/poems/48219/nikki-rosa.

Chapter 6: On and In Transition

1. A version of this passage was published in Kai M. Green, "The Essential I/Eye in We: A Black TransFeminist Approach to Ethnographic Film," *Black Camera* 6, no. 2 (Spring 2015): 187–200.

Chapter 10: On the Black Radical Tradition of Letter Writing

1. "Triggers," directed by Kai M. Green (Open TV, 2017), https://vimeo.com/221615090.
2. Faith G. Harper, *Unfuck Your Brain Workbook: Using Science to Get over Anxiety, Depression, Anger, Freak-Outs, and Triggers* (Microcosm, 2022), 24.

Chapter 11: Dear Marissa

1. A version of this piece was published on *TheSwagSpot* blog. Kai Marshall Green, letter to Marissa, TheSwagSpot, October 4, 2013, https://the-swag-spot.tumblr.com/post/63090162734/dear-marissa.

Epilogue: When, Where & How They Exit

1. Here, I reference June Jordan, "Poem about My Rights," Poetry Foundation, February 18, 2021, https://www.poetryfoundation.org/poems/48762/poem-about-my-rights.
2. Williams College consistently ranks #1 liberal arts college in the United States. "Williams College," *US News & World Report*, accessed February 22, 2021, https://www.usnews.com/best-colleges/williams-college-2229.
3. Thaai Walker, "Oakland Renames East 14th Street / It'll be 'International Blvd.,'" *SFGATE*, May 8, 1996, https://www.sfgate.com/bayarea/article/Oakland-Renames-East-14th-Street-It-ll-be-2983004.php.
4. This is a colloquialism for a place where sex workers congregate and work.
5. This is a nod to the author's dissertation "Into the Darkness: A Quare (Re)Membering of Los Angeles in a Time of Crises (1981–Present)" (University of Southern California, 2014), which is currently being revised into a book.

6. Clifford Geertz, "Deep Hanging Out," *The New York Review of Books*, October 22, 1998, https://www.nybooks.com/articles/1998/10/22/deep-hanging-out/.

7. "In 'Deep East' Oakland, youths pegged as criminals say police harassment spurs more violence," *San Francisco Public Press*, October 7, 2009, https://sfpublicpress.org/in-deep-east-oakland-youths-pegged-as-criminals-say-police-harassment-spurs-more-violence/.

8. These are the organizers, scholars, and organizations that taught me about abolition during my seven years in Los Angeles: Patrisse Khan-Cullors, cofounder of nonprofit Dignity and Power Now; Dr. Ruth Wilson Gilmore; Dr. Treva Ellison; Jermond, Jayda, Kris; A New Way of Life Reentry Project; Dr. Setsu Shigematsu, director of documentary *Re-Visions of Abolition*; Dr. Clyde Woods; Sandra Burton; Dr. Jordan Camp; Dr. Christina Heatherton; Dr. Gaye Johnson; and so many more.

9. Not an exact quote, but the ideas here are highly influenced by the "Race, Place, and Space" graduate seminar taught by Dr. Ruth Wilson Gilmore at USC.

10. Jordan, "Poem about My Rights."

11. Here, I refer to Audre Lorde, *Zami: A New Spelling of My Name* (Pandora, 1996).

12. This could have also been written "Black Queer Trans Feminist," but that would assume that Black doesn't already have the capacity to hold those identities.

13. Lorde, *Zami*, 4.

14. Lia T. Bascomb, "Water, Roads, and Mapping Diaspora through Biomythography," *Anthurium: A Caribbean Studies Journal* 14, no. 1 (2017): 10, https://doi.org/10.33596/anth.334.

15. Erica R. Edwards, "The Black President Hokum," *American Quarterly* 63, no. 1 (2011): 55.

16. C. Riley Snorton, *Black on Both Sides: A Racial History of Trans Identity* (University of Minnesota Press, 2017), 40.

17. Fred Moten, "Blackness and Nothingness (Mysticism in the Flesh)," *South Atlantic Quarterly* 112, no. 4 (October 1, 2013): 746, https://doi.org/10.1215/00382876-2345261.

18. Nadia Ellis, "Introduction: The Queer Elsewhere of Black Diaspora," in *Territories of the Soul: Queered Belonging in the Black Diaspora* (Duke University Press, 2015), 3.

19. Green, "Into the Darkness."
20. Kara Keeling, *The Witch's Flight: The Cinematic, the Black Femme, and the Image of Common Sense* (Duke University Press, 2007), 137.
21. Kai M. Green, "Troubling the Waters: Mobilizing a Trans* Analytic," in *No Tea, No Shade: New Writings in Black Queer Studies*, edited by E. Patrick Johnson (Duke University Press, 2016), 65–82.
22. Charlene A. Carruthers, *Unapologetic: A Black, Queer, and Feminist Mandate for Radical Movements* (Beacon Press, 2018); Kai M. Green, "Short Takes: Provocations on Public Feminism," *Signs: Journal of Women in Culture and Society*, n.d., http://signsjournal.org/unapologetic/.
23. Michel-Rolph Trouillot, *Silencing the Past: Power and the Production of History*, 20th ed. (Beacon Press, 2015), 2, 28–29.
24. R. J. Smith, *The Great Black Way: L.A. in the 1940s and the Lost African-American Renaissance* (PublicAffairs, 2006), 221.

About the Book Cover

1. Learn more about the artist at https://www.jamesnwelch.com/.

PHOTO © ADREINNE WAHEED

KAI MARSHALL GREEN is a writer, organizer, and educator. Green received his PhD from the University of Southern California and is assistant professor of Africana studies at the University of Delaware. An interdisciplinary scholar, he employs Black feminist theory, performance studies, and trans studies to investigate forms of self-representation and communal methods of political mobilization by Black queer folk. A founding member of Black Youth Project 100, Green has published and edited work in *GLQ: Gay and Lesbian Quarterly*, *South Atlantic Quarterly*, *Black Camera*, and *TSQ: Transgender Studies Quarterly*. *A Body Made Home* is his first book.